36017158

Making Aid Work:

Lessons from Successful Technical Cooperation in the Former Soviet Bloc

THE URBAN INSTITUTE PRESS
Washington, D.C.

THE URBAN INSTITUTE PRESS
2100 M Street, N.W.
Washington, D.C. 20037

Library of Congress Cataloging in Publication Data

Making Aid Work: Lessons from Successful Technical Cooperation in the Former Soviet Bloc / Raymond J. Struyk

1. Technical assistance—Former Soviet republics—Management.
2. Technical assistance—Europe, Eastern—Management.   3.   Economic development projects—Management.   I. Title.

HC336.27.S774   1997   96-49247
338.910947—dc21   CIP

ISBN 0-87766-658-X (paper, alk. paper)
ISBN 0-87766-657-1 (cloth, alk. paper)

Printed in the United States of America.

Distributed in North America by
University Press of America
4720 Boston Way
Lanham, MD 20706

Making Aid Work

RAYMOND J. STRUYK

THE URBAN INSTITUTE is a nonprofit policy research and educational organization established in Washington, D.C., in 1968. Its staff investigates the social and economic problems confronting the nation and public and private means to alleviate them. The Institute disseminates significant findings of its research through the publications program of its Press. The goals of the Institute are to sharpen thinking about societal problems and efforts to solve them, improve government decisions and performance, and increase citizen awareness of important policy choices.

Through work that ranges from broad conceptual studies to administrative and technical assistance, Institute researchers contribute to the stock of knowledge available to guide decision making in the public interest.

Conclusions or opinions expressed in Institute publications are those of the authors and do not necessarily reflect the views of staff members, officers or trustees of the Institute, advisory groups, or any organizations that provide financial support to the Institute.

Dedication

for Margaret McGarry Struyk

ACKNOWLEDGMENTS

I am indebted to many people over many years for the ideas expressed in this book. I have worked with and observed dozens of technical cooperation projects in the formulation stage and during implementation in Asia, Africa, and the former Soviet bloc. A significant share of these held lessons for how, in general, to carry out the business of technical cooperation in support of sector reform effectively and efficiently. Fifteen years ago Al van Huyck was among the first to convey "good practices" and a positive philosophy of technical cooperation to me.

As to the specific content of this book, my first vote of gratitude goes to Felicity Skidmore and Craig Coelen of the Urban Institute, who encouraged me to write it. Many consultants and donor officials working in the former Soviet bloc have generously shared their experience and thinking with me. Among them I single out those directing the half-dozen projects in the Russian Federation that were singled out for more careful study. Among these, James Rice was the richest source of ideas. James Norris, USAID's Mission Director in Russia, contributed thoughtful insights based on his vast experience.

Especially helpful were discussions with two Urban Institute colleagues, Katie Mark and Michael Hoffman, who have been resident advisors in Hungary and Bulgaria, respectively, for the past several years. They also carefully reviewed the draft manuscript. Michael took the time to help me develop illustrations of particular points with examples from the public administration project he directs in Bulgaria. Two anonymous reviewers of the draft manuscript offered a number of highly constructive suggestions.

Jennifer Daniel interviewed directors of a half-dozen USAID projects in the summer of 1994 and prepared insightful notes on them. Clare Romanik efficiently carried out the basic background research for chapters 1 and 2 and helped draft them, particularly chapter 2. Alice Thornton skillfully prepared the manuscript.

viii *Acknowledgments*

The Russian team members of the Housing Sector Reform Project in Russia, which I have directed since 1992, deserve special acknowledgment. They were unfailingly supportive about this work and served as an invaluable sounding board for various ideas. Among them, Nadezhda Kosareva was particularly helpful.

The Urban Institute generously supported preparation of the book from its unrestricted funds.

TABLE OF CONTENTS

Tables

FOREWORD

The Institute's Center for International Activities was established a decade and a half ago to enable the Institute to do work abroad that builds on parallel efforts in domestic policy research and evaluation. Since that time, the Institute's international focus has expanded to include a major effort to assist countries in Eastern Europe and the former Soviet Union as they traverse what Raymond Struyk has elsewhere called "the long road to the market." In *Making Aid Work*, Raymond Struyk builds on his extensive experience in technical cooperation programs in that area of the world to distill lessons for donors, project managers, and recipients of aid who wish to increase their chances of success in the technical cooperation arena.

Struyk's fundamental point is that the ultimate goal of such work should be to foster development of self-sustaining national expertise. As Ray puts it in the book, a successful technical cooperation project requires "an ability to work hard planning for the project's own obsolescence—by strengthening local analysts, administrators, and institutions to replace the project at its conclusion."

In 1995 this goal was achieved in the Russian Federation with creation of the Institute of Urban Economics. This is a nonprofit organization founded by a highly qualified team of Russian specialists who had trained and worked together for three years under Urban Institute auspices. The goals of the new organization are to develop and implement new approaches to solving problems in housing policy, housing and urban infrastructure financing, and urban land use.

Struyk's lessons are drawn not only from his own experiences but also from those of other technical cooperation efforts in the newly independent states. He includes a rich collection of case study evidence, which lends force and conviction to the points he makes. It is my hope that others may benefit from the insights Struyk brings to his discussion and that the corpus of technical cooperation efforts in the area does indeed yield an ever stronger infrastructure of domestic human and institutional capital around the world.

William Gorham
President

Part One

LAYING THE GROUNDWORK

Chapter One

TECHNICAL COOPERATION: COMPLEX WORK

Foreign assistance is a controversial topic, to judge by the acrimonious debate about it within Congress and the amount of energy the Administration spends year after year to secure funding. In 1995 the House of Representatives, led by its Republican freshman and sophomore classes, voted major funding cuts and the merging of three specialized federal agencies in the foreign affairs complex with the State Department.[1] At the same time, members such as Lee Hamilton of Indiana, Henry Hyde of Illinois, and Doug Bereuter of Nebraska tried to stem the rising tide of isolationism (Greenberger, 1995). Powerful congressional figures like Senator Jesse Helms routinely attack the foreign aid program as ineffective and wasteful, while equally powerful members such as Senators Thomas Daschle, Richard Lugar, and John Kerry find merit in these expenditures and argue for maintaining foreign aid if not increasing it to the levels of earlier years.[2]

Foreign aid has numerous parts, including humanitarian aid, in-kind assistance such as food transfers, funds to help with macroeconomic stability, and technical cooperation programs. The complaints often concentrate on the last category: programs that aim to improve the effectiveness of government institutions and programs or likewise help the private sector, such as the restructuring of banks and enterprises in Central and Eastern Europe. These programs require the delivery of expert advice and close work with local counterpart individuals and agencies. To be successful the tasks have to be done very well and the client has to be receptive to the advice and willing to make changes—a combination that has been exceedingly difficult to realize in practice.

In the case of the United States, the task of managing aid programs falls primarily to the U.S. Agency for International Development (USAID). All bilateral donors have similar agencies and the European Union has a large bureaucracy to manage its programs for Eastern Europe (PHARE) and the Newly Independent States (TACIS). Without exception these agencies find themselves under pressure from their governments to have more success stories to report.[3]

Senator Helms and like thinkers in other countries receive help episodically in their efforts to portray foreign assistance as wasteful and ineffective (and therefore not deserving of funding) from journalists who write stories about the high living and lack of productivity of consultants engaged to provide expert advice to recipient countries. Typical of these is the article in the October 16, 1995, *International Herald Tribune*, in which Justin Keay reported:

> Whether advising on privatization in Poland, suggesting how best to reform Hungary's banking system or revamping Romania's tourist industry, consultants have been in the front line of the West's efforts to help post-Communist Europe help itself.
>
> But where they were once welcome as saviors imbued with special knowledge, they are now increasingly reviled as overpaid—an average daily rate for a Western consultant in the region is 1,000 European Currency Units ($1,315)—ill-informed or underequipped to deal with the problems.
>
> Resentment has been fueled by the knowledge that this army eats into the West's aid programs—taking up as much as 40 percent of last year's 2 billion Ecus disbursed by PHARE, the EU's assistance program for Eastern Europe—and its soldiers rarely stay in one place, prompting critics to use the phrase "consultancy tourism." (p. 11)

A February 1994 *Wall Street Journal* article about U.S. assistance to Russia sounded a similar theme:

> . . . With cash-starved Russians trying to jump-start their fledgling businesses and economy—and antireform politicians gaining ground—"we don't need 90% of 'technical assistance' money going to American experts," says Aleksander A. Jlnikov, head of a Russian commission coordinating foreign aid.
>
> Some U.S. policy experts share those concerns. Marshall Goldman, a Russia specialist and professor at Wellesley College, recently told the Senate Banking Committee that Russian aid in the hands of U.S. consultants and "beltway bandits" benefits Russians "minimally, if at all." He added, "I look for a scandal down the road that's going to upset the American taxpayer."[4,5]

Even the generally positive 1995 article by Fred Hiatt and Daniel Southerland on assistance to Russia included the following critique:

> . . . as the aid program swelled to more than $1 billion last year, the political desire to show support for Russia out-stripped U.S. bureaucrats' ability to dole out aid sensibly and Russian reformers' ability to

absorb it, according to people familiar with the program. As a result, more and more money went to American consultants with generous overheads and travel budgets and little knowledge of the Russian scene, and to Russian bureaucrats with little appetite for reform.[6]

Of course, there are success stories, some striking, to balance the criticisms, among them those of small grassroots projects cited by Hiatt and Southerland. But even among proponents there is a sense that improved performance must be possible, that better organization or a different philosophy will yield visibly enhanced achievement. "High living" consultants would receive less attention if the impact of their work were greater and more visible to recipient country officials and its business community, as well as to outside observers.

This book is about how to improve the performance of technical cooperation programs in Eastern Europe and the Newly Independent States of the former Soviet Union. (Below I typically refer to these countries as the former Soviet bloc.) Fundamentally, the objective of the book is to lessen the dependence of project success on a brilliant performance by the chief-of-party by retailing a set of practical steps for donors, project managers, and recipients of aid.

I have deliberately restricted the topic to a single facet of foreign aid in a limited region, because technical cooperation programs in this region differ fundamentally from those in Asia, Africa, and Latin America, and because of the urgency of the work in this region from the perspective of the principal Western nations.

Conceptually and practically one can divide the task of providing assistance to any country among strategy, tactics, and execution. With respect to strategy, numerous statements have been made about what type of assistance might be provided to the countries of the former Soviet bloc, the goals of such assistance, and the extent to which bilateral assistance should be altruistic or self-interested. The "trade versus aid" debate falls into this category. Tactical discussion focuses on what could work in practice and what is affordable. If economic stabilization is determined to be the foremost objective, are donors' funds better invested in a currency stabilization fund or advice to the Central Bank, the Ministry of Finance, and the Office of the Prime Minister?

Execution, the third level, is the subject of this book. To take a military analogy, after the generals have mapped out the strategy and the division commanders have determined the tactics of the battle, it is up to the battalion and company commanders to create success on the ground. In the present context, given that a donor has decided to provide technical assistance in a particular sector in Eastern Europe or the former Soviet Union, what lessons have been learned about how to increase the likelihood of success? Execution is fundamental. If the troops on the ground fail to deliver, the best strategy and tactics are meaningless.

The subject I address is how to improve the return on investment in sectoral technical cooperation or assistance programs. By "sectoral" I mean blocks of economic activity such as the agriculture, housing, transportation, banking, energy, health, and education sectors. This definition excludes macroeconomic restructuring. Thus, the productivity of advisors stationed at the Central Bank, for example, is beyond my purview.

The boundaries of sectors can be flexibly defined for the case at hand. The main point is that sectoral projects work with whole blocks of activity—reforming the health sector, not only hospitals; the agricultural sector, not just rural credit. The advantage of working at the sector level is that the project is much more likely to address the core policy issues. A rural credit project could be undermined by a government policy of price controls for farm products. Farmers could have a severely limited ability to pay market interest rates for credit because the prices for their products are restricted. Without addressing price controls, the credit project has a major problem in pushing for market interest rates.

Despite several years of experience in the region, many sector reform technical cooperation projects are patently wasteful. The efficiency with which millions of dollars are spent on technical cooperation projects could be measurably increased. This may seem unimportant at a time in which USAID is talking about wrapping up its assistance to some Eastern European nations. Far from it. While USAID is "graduating" a few of the most advanced countries, many countries to the east and south, particularly the republics of the former Soviet Union outside the Baltics, will need a minimum of several more years of assistance with sectoral reform. The unexpected difficulty of economic transformation is the one truth in this region upon which everyone agrees. Moreover, while the U.S. may wish to view its role as relatively short term, some other bilateral donors and the European Community see providing assistance as a longer-run task. For some countries in Eastern Europe the European Union sees its task as helping prepare them for accession to the Union. In short, the stakes are high to the donors seeking to improve efficiency of sector reform in the former Soviet bloc. The stakes are clearly even higher to the recipient countries, who badly need to improve the efficiency of their social, economic, productive, and industrial sectors.

TECHNICAL COOPERATION IN AID TO THE FORMER SOVIET BLOC

I begin with a discussion of the evolution of technical cooperation programs and then examine their prominence and composition in the total assistance packages to the former Soviet bloc. The terms "technical cooperation" and "technical assistance" are often used interchangeably by practitioners. Technical cooperation is used throughout this book to emphasize the positive contributions officials and other professionals in the recipient country should be making in donor-initiated sector reform projects.

Technical What?

Until 15 years ago, technical cooperation as bilateral assistance mostly involved individual training programs and student exchanges. The most widely used practice of technical cooperation in the World Bank was providing training to individuals responsible for executing feasibility studies for investment projects. In the 1980s, however, there was "disappointment experienced by some agencies that merely training certain individuals has failed to bring about substantial strengthening and self-reliance of the agencies or institutions involved" (Muscat 1986: 82–83). This caused rethinking about the purpose and context of technical cooperation. The Bank and other aid deliverers recognized that technical cooperation is more effectively delivered in a sectoral framework. For example, Muscat (1986: 83) on the British case states: "The position of the Overseas Development Administration is particularly instructive in this area, since the UK traditionally has financed a large programme of fellowship training, but now sees a need to rationalize its aid around 'sectoral' objectives." Similarly, a 1982 World Bank review of program performance stated that "institutional or other development objectives at the project level are increasingly linked to wider sector objectives as both the Bank and the borrowers have become aware that the effectiveness of projects and of institutions which they help to establish or to strengthen, often depends on a sector environment supportive of these objectives."[7]

We define sectoral technical cooperation as a comprehensive, co-ordinated set of activities carried out jointly with the cooperating country that are designed to improve the efficiency with which a sector operates and possibly improve the equity with which services provided by the sector are distributed. A sectoral technical coopera-tion program may be composed of several different projects that ad-dress different problems, as long as they have complementary sectoral objectives.

This definition is consistent with statements of major donors. The Development Assistance Council of the OECD, in its *Principles for New Orientations in Technical Co-operation*, sets forth as one prin-ciple to "stress the essential importance for effective Technical Co-operation of improved planning in the context of co-ordinated support for sectoral objectives and policies and, in particular, use of a pro-gramme rather than a project-by-project approach" (DAC/OECD 1991: 5). The World Bank categorizes technical cooperation as either engi-neering or institutional; the proportion of Bank technical cooperation directed toward the latter type has been increasing since the 1980s (Buyck 1991: v). Institutional technical cooperation is closely related to our definition of sectoral technical cooperation. According to the authors of a World Bank document, institutional technical cooperation:

> consists of (a) diagnostic and prescriptive assistance such as advice on institutional or policy matters and studies for national economic man-agement and planning, public administration, or the management and operation of a particular sector and entity; and (b) managerial, techni-cal, or other direct operational support as well as staff training (Lethem and Cooper 1983: 1).

Deliverers of technical cooperation may work primarily with a branch of the government or with enterprises in the private sector. The USAID privatization program in Central and Eastern Europe pro-vides an example of different emphases and partners that together create a comprehensive approach. Among the categories of assistance provided under this program are (1) assistance at the policy/program level; (2) assistance to government agencies; (3) specialized transac-tional support; and (4) firm-specific assistance. Under the first three categories consultants work primarily with the government to create the appropriate policies and to build the institutional capacity for and facilitate the implementation of those policies. The fourth category, in contrast, focuses on a particular firm and its privatization strategy.[8]

To promote sector reform in the former Soviet bloc, I believe a sectoral technical cooperation program must address five key areas.

1. Development of legislation and implementing regulations. Reform means changing old ways of doing things. The former Soviet bloc enshrined a particular organization of activity in detailed laws and regulations. Reform is simply impossible without replacing or modifying the inherited legal framework. New laws and new regulations require new thinking about policy. And it is here that outsiders can provide extraordinarily valuable assistance, i.e., by defining the new policy *in the specific context of the country,* and then working in detail with those drafting the new legislation to convey the ideas accurately. This is only partially the task of a lawyer; it is more importantly a task of experienced policy analysts.

2. Demonstration projects. Experts who have worked in Eastern Europe on sector reform have had the experience of standing in front of a room of career civil servants, trying to explain a new idea, and finding polite but uncomprehending faces before them. I once tried to explain to a group of officials charged with maintaining the municipal housing in the large Russian city of Nizhni Novgorod that in order to improve maintenance, the city administration had agreed to hold competitions among private and public firms for a contract to maintain several thousand units in each of several packages. The municipal firms that had enjoyed monopolies on maintaining packages of buildings could compete, but the monopoly was over. Naturally, there was anger. But mostly there was just disbelief that such a system could work. In this particular case, we had the example of a successful demonstration project in Moscow. We were able to use this as our credential, but without it, the necessary cooperation would almost certainly not have been achieved.

This is a general truth. Experience has shown that in the former Soviet bloc, if you want to induce many cities or hospitals or banks to change the way they conduct their activities, you must convince them with a live example. Demonstration projects are the live examples.

3. Monitoring and evaluation. It sounds obvious. If you are working on reforming the agricultural sector, you had better keep very well informed, systematically informed, of developments in the sector—changes in the law, introduction of innovations, changes in general practices. Moreover, if your project has succeeded in changing laws or regulations, you will want to know what the effects have been, so you can correct problems, if necessary, or use the results as leverage in the next round of negotiations for further change. This activity, obvious as it may be, is often missing in sectoral reform projects.

4. Dissemination. Getting the word out about positive changes occurring in the sector is a way of encouraging more administrators in other locations to undertake similar changes. The range of possibilities is nearly endless and well known—mass distribution of brochures to professionals, working with ministries on the publication of "official guidelines," participation in conferences, articles in the trade press, jointly sponsoring conferences with others, mass media events such as public service announcements on TV, or producing draft newspaper stories to be supplied to local papers. Some vehicles work better for some sectors and some are more typically used in certain countries. But to ignite widespread change, "advertising" and informing are essential in any context.

5. *Institutionalization.* Few reforms are on-off affairs. Rather, a policy reform breakthrough is made—the legislation is passed—then the long road of implementation begins. Similarly, a demonstration may succeed in, for example, certain local water companies or polyclinics, but dozens of utilities and hundreds of additional clinics will need help, if they are to introduce the new practices after the technical cooperation program is gone. A key goal of the technical cooperation program should be to perpetuate those elements of its work for which there is a demand. Examples include training courses offered by local institutions on a fee basis, consulting services provided by a local institution on a commercial basis, or creation of staff in a government office (local, regional, or national) charged with helping service deliverers change their procedures or introduce new activities.

The easiest way to convince oneself of the necessity of including all these elements is to ask what happens if any one of them is missing from a project. If no monitoring is done, for example, what could be the consequences? Your team will be less effective in drafting legislation and regulations because they will not be informed about shifts in sentiment for or against a provision. If you have implemented a demonstration program and have no hard information on its performance, selling the idea to skeptical national and local leaders will be nearly impossible; even with hard evaluation results, you may not succeed. Real evaluation is novel in the region and hard figures can carry real weight; without this component the project is working under a handicap.

The Volume of Technical Cooperation Assistance

Beginning from the perspective of the total aid program, I define four principal types of assistance:

1. emergency, humanitarian assistance, such as food and medical supplies;
2. balance of payments and convertibility support and assistance with external debt management (Barre et al. 1992: 73);
3. technical cooperation that provides infrastructure support, institution development and capacity building, and, particularly, training and policy advice (Assaf 1994: 243); and
4. project investment in the form of international loans in support of medium-term infrastructure investment (European Commission 1995: 3).

Humanitarian assistance responds when war, natural disaster, or economic and social breakdown jeopardize people's lives. Experience has shown that humanitarian assistance can often be delivered efficiently and cost-effectively by charitable or private/volunteer organizations. One benefit of using organizations such as these, which are typically smaller, is that they deliver assistance directly to the beneficiaries. A grant to Project HOPE to deliver donated emergency medical supplies to hospitals in the Newly Independent States is an example. The program's auditors noted that "the recipients (hospital personnel) were also grateful that the products were delivered directly to them and not through a government agency like the Ministry of Health" (Regional Inspector General. 1994: 5). While the principal aim of humanitarian assistance is to reduce human misery, it can also help decision-makers channel energy toward long-term transformative goals instead of being captured by the demands of immediate subsistence needs.

Balance of payments and convertibility support address the macroeconomic stabilization of a country. An institution like the International Monetary Fund (IMF) is usually responsible for devising a stabilization strategy and disbursing funds. As a prerequisite for release of funds, IMF officials agree on macroeconomic goals with the government. Achievement of these goals depends largely upon the political will of the country's leaders. The goals do not include the transformation and restructuring of the economy, but rather attempt to create an environment in which it will be possible to begin the stabilization process.

Technical cooperation and project investment aim to transform and restructure particular social, economic, production, and industrial sectors of the country that is in transition. The technical assistance aspect involves "building the institutional, legal and regulatory infrastructure underpinning a modern market economy" (CCET/OECD

1994: 2). The project investment aspect involves providing the funds to upgrade the country's physical and technical infrastructure.

Much sector aid to Central and Eastern Europe (CEE) has been in the form of technical cooperation. In the education and public administration sectors, technical cooperation constituted four-fifths of the total aid over the 1990–1994 period (table 1.1). In the health, environment, agriculture, and other social and economic infrastructure sectors, technical cooperation accounted for more than one-third. Only in the sectors demanding a very high level of physical infrastructure development—such as transport, communications, and energy—did technical cooperation account for less than 10 percent of the total aid provided for the sector. Even so, sector technical cooperation constituted only about 9 percent of total aid to the region during the 1990–1994 period, because physical infrastructure projects, when they occur, are so huge.

Table 1.1 G-24 TECHNICAL COOPERATION COMMITMENTS TO CENTRAL AND EASTERN EUROPE BY SECTOR (JANUARY 1, 1990–DECEMBER 31, 1994) (Unit: Million ECU)

Sector	Total Assistance	Technical Cooperation	Technical Cooperation as Percent of Total
Education	1,006	821	81.7
Public Administration	355	287	80.8
Environment	1,243	621	50.0
Health	499	238	47.8
Other Economic Sectors	773	353	45.6
Agriculture	1,432	569	39.7
Other Social Sectors	999	363	36.3
Industry	3,351	740	22.1
Trade, Banking & Tourism	1,596	339	21.2
Other Production Sectors	195	39	19.7
Energy	2,224	158	7.1
Transport	2,985	193	6.5
Multisector	21,184	627	3.0
Communications	1,603	32	2.0
Non-sectoral assistance	35,262	1,348	3.8
TOTAL	74,707	6,728	9.0

Note: Nonsectoral assistance includes macroeconomic assistance, structural adjustment assistance, debt reorganization, food aid, emergency assistance, support for Private Voluntary Organizations and unallocated or unspecified assistance. CEE countries include Albania, Bulgaria, the Czech Republic, Estonia, Hungary, Latvia, Lithuania, Poland, Romania, the Slovak Republic, Slovenia, and the former Yugoslav Republic of Macedonia. On 30 January 1996, 1 ECU was equal to $1.23.
Source: European Commission Directorate General IA. March 1995. *Scoreboard of Assistance Commitments to the Countries of Central and Eastern Europe, 1990–1994.*

Once stabilization and technical cooperation programs have begun to build up financial and institutional capacity, a country can become eligible for physical infrastructure and project loans from international financial institutions and individual countries. Before this stage is reached, donors may have legitimate doubts about whether the country is able to service the loans, and recipients may lack the information to know whether they really need them.

The record of the G-24 group of countries' assistance to Central and Eastern Europe from 1990 through 1994 attests to this order of aid priorities. In the first stage, macro-financial assistance and debt reorganization represented the largest share of aid by far. In the year 1991, for example, these two categories of aid constituted more than twice the funds of all the other categories (emergency aid, technical cooperation, project investment and other) combined. Emergency humanitarian assistance became larger and then stayed relatively constant as more needy countries were consistently added to the beneficiary pool. Technical cooperation to the region was highest in 1992 and 1993, once other forms of aid had provided some financial and economic stability. Technical cooperation, in turn, built institutional capacity, which made it possible for physical infrastructure loans to be productive. From 1990 to 1994, project investment in Central and Eastern Europe was at its highest levels in the last two years (European Commission 1995: 5).

Assistance can be provided through the following vehicles: (1) cash grant assistance; (2) in-kind grant assistance; and (3) loans or lines of credit. Assistance for balance of payments and convertibility support is usually provided in the form of loans, lines of credit, or forgiveness of loans. The latter category was very important in the assistance package to Poland in the early 1990s. Emergency humanitarian assistance is often in the form of in-kind grant assistance such as food or medical supplies. Donors also provide cash grants and loans to purchase the necessary supplies for such assistance. The primary vehicles for project investment are loans; however, the projects will often have a supplementary technical cooperation package, which may be paid for by a loan or a grant. Technical cooperation projects that stand alone are most often financed partially or fully by grants, depending on the donor and the capacity of the beneficiary to pay for the services.

The grant component of G-24 assistance to Central and Eastern Europe from 1990 to 1994 was less than the loans or lines of credit component.[9] Grant aid peaked at 36 percent in 1992, but in 1994 represented 26 percent of overall assistance provided to the countries of Central and Eastern Europe (European Commission 1995: 6). If the loans from the international financial institutions are excluded, grants composed 40 percent of the assistance provided from 1990 through 1994.

The share of grant assistance provided by G-24 countries to the countries of Central and Eastern Europe varies widely by donor country (table 1.2). Four out of the 15 major donors (countries that committed more than 500 million ECU equivalent [$615 million[10]] to the region from 1990–1994) provided more than half their funds in grant assistance: Denmark, Canada, the United States, and the Netherlands. Most of the other countries provided between one-fourth and one-half of their aid package in grants. Spain, the United Kingdom, and Japan provided a smaller share of their aid in grant assistance. In total, the European Union provided over 13 billion ECU ($16 billion) in grant assistance, 38.7 percent of its total aid package (European Commis-

Table 1.2 G-24 GRANT ASSISTANCE COMMITMENTS TO CENTRAL AND EASTERN EUROPE BY DONOR (JANUARY 1, 1990–DECEMBER 31, 1994) (Unit: Million ECU)

Donor	Total Assistance	Grant Assistance	Grants as Percent of Total
Denmark	886	655	73.9
Canada	1,713	1,184	69.1
EU Programmes	8,390	5,642	67.2
United States	9,575	5,494	57.4
Netherlands	1,145	573	50.1
France	5,512	2,248	40.8
Italy	1,464	536	36.6
Austria	2,267	692	30.5
Finland	696	210	30.2
Sweden	1,390	405	29.2
Germany	11,239	3,138	27.9
Norway	569	154	27.0
Switzerland	1,605	403	25.1
Japan	3,127	595	19.0
United Kingdom	794	117	14.7
Spain	1,041	7	0.7
TOTAL	51,413	22,053	42.9

Note: Includes commitments only from major donors (those that committed more than 500 million ECU). Excludes assistance from smaller donors and multilateral lending institutions (the latter do not provide grant assistance). CEE countries include Albania, Bulgaria, the Czech Republic, Estonia, Hungary, Latvia, Lithuania, Poland, Romania, the Slovak Republic, Slovenia, and the former Yugoslav Republic of Macedonia. On 30 January 1996, 1 ECU was equal to $1.23.

Source: European Commission Directorate General IA. March 1995. *Scoreboard of Assistance Commitments to the Countries of Central and Eastern Europe, 1990–1994.*

sion 1995: 13). According to Hutchings (1994: 185) one of the strengths of the U.S. programs is their reliance on grant assistance rather than loans or lines of credit.

Other decisions involved in creating an overall aid strategy include the composition of the assistance package and the speed with which it is delivered. Rapidity of disbursement is commonly viewed as one measure of the efficiency of an aid program. The United States has focused on economic growth and private sector development, whereas the EU's preference has been for "social market" programs in public infrastructure, industrial restructuring, and social welfare (Hutchings 1994: 185). The American government's decision to focus more on the private sector has allowed it to deliver aid more quickly than other major donor countries. According to a letter from the Department of State in response to a GAO report, this approach has left the United States disburse funds at about twice the rate of the EU (GAO 1992: 42). This may be an overstatement. Doubtlessly, differences in contract administration procedures are also important.

The nations of the former Soviet Union have also received significant aid from the West for technical cooperation (table 1.3). In general, the data on assistance to these countries are less well organized than those for Central and Eastern Europe. Even so, the aggregate figures

Table 1.3 TECHNICAL COOPERATION TO THE FORMER SOVIET UNION BY DONOR (SEPTEMBER 1, 1990–DECEMBER 31, 1994)
(Unit: ECU million)

Donor	Total Assistance	Technical Cooperation	Technical Cooperation as Percent of Total
European Union	4,495	1,798	40.0
Member States[a]	9,433	353	3.7
Germany	41,510	468	1.1
EFTA[b]	1,363	159	11.7
Canada	1,583	117	7.4
United States	14,134	2,098	14.8
Japan	4,782	141	2.9
Total	77,300	5,134	6.6

Note: This table does not include assistance to the Baltic countries. On 30 January 1996, 1 ECU was equal to $1.23.
a. Bilateral assistance from all members of the European Union except Germany. Germany is enumerated separately because of its large level of assistance.
b. European Free Trade Association. During this period its members included Austria, Iceland, Norway, Finland, Sweden, and Switzerland.
Source: European Commission Directorate General IA. October 1995. *Towards Greater Economic Integration: The European Union's Financial Assistance and Trade Policy for Central and Eastern Europe and the Newly Independent States.*

convey important information. For 1990–1994, the CEE countries received ECU 6.7 billion and the FSU nations ECU 5.1 billion in technical assistance funding—or ECU 61 and ECU 18 on a per capita basis, respectively.[11] Over the five-year period, donors' average contribution for technical assistance to the combined region was ECU 2.3 billion. These are substantial amounts year in and year out. In both the CEE and FSU countries, the programs of the European Union, Germany, and the United States have been the largest.

THE STAKES IN IMPROVING PERFORMANCE

Given these substantial amounts, donors certainly have an interest in improving the productivity of funds spent on technical cooperation projects. In an era of fixed or declining aid budgets, doing more with less is a commonly stated imperative.

But the gains from better designed and executed projects go well beyond the money involved. Badly performing projects are a drag on further reform. First, good projects can accelerate the transition process. Poorly designed and executed projects can impede it. Failure of a demonstration program at the municipal level designed to show the virtues of replacing state provision of services with private sources may well make municipal and national officials wary of trying this approach again. Unproductive projects that place significant time demands on senior local officials will make these same officials reluctant to invite more foreign advisors to their cities or ministries.

Second, poorly performing projects produce problems for donor agencies as well because failure to produce results inevitably reduces the enthusiasm and interest in supporting technical cooperation. For this reason alone donors also want to see demonstrable progress. This is particularly the case in the former Soviet bloc, where the view was that the transition would be short and quick assistance decisive. While the donors may realize they were overly optimistic at the outset of the transition, they still sense that real progress should be evident from their investment in these countries.

Last, there are significant potential benefits to future recipient countries from "getting the technical cooperation model right."

NEWS FROM THE FRONT

To extend the military analogy, this book is a dispatch from the front lines. From the perspective of a seasoned implementer of technical cooperation projects in Hungary and the Russian Federation, as well as several Asian countries previously, the objective of the book is to lay out clearly the lessons learned for structuring a successful program. Stated alternatively, my goal is to lessen the dependence of program success on good luck and a particularly strong performance by the chief-of-party implementing the program.

The lessons are for both the donor community (i.e., those individuals at USAID, the European Union's PHARE and TACIS programs, the British Know How Fund, and others who define and manage technical cooperation programs) and for the firms and individuals who actually implement the programs. I realize that donor agencies' behavior is substantially determined by the legislatures, governments, and commissions to which they are responsible. Therefore, the lessons are addressed to them as well.

I do not address explicitly possible changes in the contracting and management procedures employed by the donor agencies. As might be expected, these procedures differ substantially among donors. I am acutely aware that bureaucratic rules and an agency's imperative to control the technical cooperation process may thwart giving contractors greater freedom of action or defining individual projects more broadly so as to encompass more of the five elements in a successful program. I hope that my statement of the lessons is sufficiently clear that the specific administrative changes needed for their realization can be readily deduced.

THE FUNDAMENTALS

Donors and contractors are being less effective than they could easily be in conducting technical cooperation projects in the former Soviet bloc aimed at moving economic sectors to the market. The most inept practices include:

Small, typically disconnected short-term projects, whose overall impact is less than the sum of the parts. Programs should include the five elements outlined above and have a realistic life span—years, not months. And best performance is much more likely when a single contractor is responsible and a single donor is managing (and funding) the project.

Poor use of expertise developed during the project design stage when going to project implementation, which handicaps implementation efforts unduly. Most donors have strong rules prohibiting firms, and in some cases individuals, that help design a project from being part of the implementation team. While the desire to create a "level playing field" for firms competing for the implementation contract is laudable, it comes at a high price.

Little imagination in structuring real dialogues between the donors and host country officials in designing projects, with the result that the officials are not strongly committed. Predictably, projects with such antecedents often have lackluster records, even when a strong implementation team is fielded. Real discussions facilitated by the donor can establish in advance the broad boundaries of the work and highlight examples of project components to make the dialogue concrete.

Too little use of local professionals, which makes projects cost more and reduces their effectiveness. Merely having local professionals on staff is not enough. They should be assigned real responsibility as soon as they possess the necessary skills, and the staffing pattern of projects should be consciously and consistently in the direction of substituting local for Western professionals.

Too slow start-up and too many Phase 1 tasks, which reduce the odds of attaining early credibility. Projects have a much better chance of succeeding if they are organized to start quickly but on a limited number of tasks. Such a strategy increases credibility early in the project with senior host country officials and "service deliverers" (bankers, hospital officials, local government administrators, teachers). Once these credentials are established, branching out into additional areas is comparatively easy, as there will be committed support for the initiatives.

The subject of this book is how to convert inept practices such as those implied in the foregoing into those that will be more effective.

MY CREDENTIALS

My experience as the resident project manager for the Housing Sector Reform Program in the Russian Federation from early 1992 through the writing of this book in 1996 is the primary basis for my observations. This program was carried out by the Urban Institute under contract with USAID. The project was formally evaluated by the U.S. Government Accounting Office in 1994 and rated a clear success in terms of both impact and cost-effectiveness (GAO 1995a). In subsequent reviews by USAID it also received positive marks.

This experience is supplemented with additional information from a review of several other sector technical cooperation programs being implemented in Russia,[12] two earlier years of on-the-ground experience in housing sector reform in Hungary, and discussions on technical cooperation projects with Americans and local staff implementing such projects in the region but outside Russia. I also draw on more general information I acquired during the 15 years before I began work in Hungary—when I was an active consultant in a dozen developing countries, observed scores of technical cooperation projects, and followed the literature on the lessons garnered from conducting such projects.

That most of my examples of success come from the Housing Sector Reform Program does not imply that I regard it as uniquely successful.[13] There are indeed many other solid projects completed and ongoing in the region. I simply know the housing project best.

Are the lessons I draw from the examples I highlight here applicable to projects in economic sectors other than housing? Yes. The five components of a comprehensive technical cooperation project listed earlier certainly apply across sectors, even though the relative emphasis on each will vary significantly with the specific sector and country. In addition, my lessons apply to the *process of carrying out the assignment*, not the technical composition. I address ways to engage local professionals effectively in projects; ways to structure training programs so that they have better chances of continuing to be offered after donor support is withdrawn; and how to create positive incentives to local officials to adopt reforms—a near precondition for getting reforms to move beyond the pilot stage. None of these points is sector-specific.

THE HOUSING SECTOR REFORM PROGRAM IN BRIEF

Although the lessons are not restricted to the housing sector, the experience of the Housing Sector Reform Program (HSRP) is so central to the presentation that I think it useful, for context, to provide a thumbnail sketch of the program as it existed in the summer of 1995. (A more complete description appears in Annex A.)

The U.S. Agency for International Development signed agreements in March 1992 with the Russian Federation and the cities of Moscow, Novosibirsk, and Ekaterinburg, and with the Oblast (regional government) of Nizhni Novgorod in November 1993. Resident advisors were assigned to all three cities. The Urban Institute carried out the program for USAID with the Russian Federation, Moscow, the Nizhni Novgorod Oblast, and cities in Central Russia.

The Urban Institute began its work in March 1992 and has had resident advisors present since August 1992. The project team is centrally located in Moscow, making frequent visits to other cities. The project began small, with two U.S. and two Russian professionals. In the mature phase of the project, the 25 Russian professionals outnumber Americans six to one.

The principal activities of the Urban Institute program—upon which this book draws—were three:

1. *Acting as the principal advisor to government on housing reform legislation.* In addition to working on the Law on Fundamentals of Housing Policy in the Russian Federation (passed December 1992) and the numerous regulations implementing this law, the team, for example, drafted Moscow's regulations on condominiums (the first in the country) and has strongly influenced the content of the Law on Mortgage, which will create the essential legal basis for housing lending.

2. *Carrying out a series of demonstration projects.* The objective was to create the concrete examples essential to widespread adoption of significant change.

(a) Introduction of competitive, private maintenance for municipal housing. In March 1993, three private firms took over management of 2,000 rental units in one Moscow region, following a competitive procurement process. A second group of 5,000 was placed under management in September of the same year. The results of a rigorous evaluation of the experience of these projects showed that maintenance improved sharply and at no additional cost. By December 1995 Moscow had expanded the program to cover 325,000 units. Mayor Yuri Luzhkov issued a decree in June 1995 requiring the entire municipal housing stock to be placed under private maintenance within three years. Competitions to select maintenance firms for municipal housing have taken place with Urban Institute help in Nizhni Novgorod, Bor, Arzamas, Vladimir, Ryazan, Petrozavorsk, and other cities.

(b) Raising rents and implementing housing allowances. On the basis of Federation legislation, the City of Moscow enacted a program of significant rent increases combined with the introduction of housing allowances in November 1993. The design of the program, which was implemented in August 1994, was based on simulations conducted by the Urban Institute team. The team also assisted in development of a detailed procedures manual for administration of the program; this manual has been disseminated by the Ministry of Construction (Minstroi) as guidance to all administrations in the country. The Urban Institute team has worked with Minstroi to prepare instructions to local governments on administrative improvements (including verification of applicant income, quality control, and preparation of performance reports for senior city managers).

(c) Introducing condominiums. Beginning in the spring of 1994, the Institute team has been working with about 20 cities, mostly in central Russia, to help them create the necessary regulatory basis for the creation of condominiums in the city. The program includes working out local legislative documents and training local professionals to work with homeowner groups who wish to create a condominium association. The team helps establish early associations. This includes providing guidance on the contracting for maintenance and management services. Working with the Academy of International Entrepreneurism, a training program for local officials and condominium leaders has been developed and is offered every several months.

(d) Long-term mortgage lending. Helping establish long-term mortgage lending is the largest component of the technical cooperation program. Under a November 1992 agreement between USAID and Mosbusinessbank, Russia's third largest commercial bank, the team provided intensive assistance to prepare the bank to make financially responsible mortgage loans. The bank initiated lending in May 1994. Assistance involved all phases of operations (legal documentation, underwriting, and loan servicing, including development of the necessary software; loan instrument development; and risk management).

The Urban Institute team is working with about 20 additional banks to help them begin or expand mortgage lending. More than half are already making such loans. The banks include Stolichni Bank, Tveruniversal, Sokol Bank (Cherprovets), East Siberian

Commercial Bank (Irkusk), Inkombank, Pskovakobank, and St. Petersburg Ipoteke Bank.

The materials developed under this assistance program are made available to other banks through the production of the "Mortgage Handbook" series, which facilitates other banks beginning operations.

The Institute also works with the Association of Mortgage Banks and the Association of Commercial Banks-Russia to offer a comprehensive training program in mortgage lending. The first course was presented in February 1994, and in 1995 five different courses were offered with a total of 10 offerings. Faculty for most courses was at first a combination of Russian and American experts and later generally exclusively Russian.

3. Monitoring and evaluation. This is an active program to document the changes in the sector, including a series of surveys, and the impacts of the work in the project. Several rigorous evaluations of the project-supported demonstrations have been conducted as part of this effort.

Notes

1. This provision, contained in the "American Overseas Interest Act," of June 8, 1995, applied to the Agency for International Development, the U.S. Information Agency, and the Arms Control and Disarmament Agency. In any event, the Senate authorization bill, passed on December 14, 1995, authorized the President to submit a reorganization plan for accomplishing the tasks then performed by the three agencies and achieving very substantial gains in the efficiency of their operations. If the President *does not submit* a plan, the organizations will be abolished. The authorization bill was passed in April 1996 but vetoed by the President. Nevertheless, the Administrator of USAID, Brian Atwood, announced plans for major restructuring and downsizing of the Agency in March, as described in T. W. Lippman, "It's a Smaller World After Budget Shrinkage," *The Washington Post*, March 21, 1996, p. A-15.

2. For Senator Daschle's views, for example, see Daschle (1996). Where the American public stands on foreign aid is far from clear, as indicated by the somewhat inconsistent results from public opinion polls. Interestingly, according to a 1994 poll, the average American believes that 15 percent of the U.S. budget goes for foreign aid versus the 1 percent in fact. For details, see Kull (1995).

3. See U.S. General Accounting Office (1995b: 2, 51). [NSIAD-95-37].

4. John Fiakla, "Helping Ourselves: U.S. Aid to Russia Is a Windfall For U.S. Consultants, but Russians Feel Left Out," February 24, 1994.

5. For a less temperate critique of U.S. aid to Russia, see Waller (1996).

6. "Grass Roots Aid Works Best in Russia: Many Large U.S. Projects Support Bureaucracies, Consultants," *The Washington Post*, February 12, 1995, pp. A1, A36.

7. Quoted in Cassen (1994: 161).

8. Development Economics Group/Louis Berger International and Checchi and Company (1993: 6–7).

9. The conceptual distinction between cash grant assistance and in-kind grant assistance has collapsed these categories into one grant assistance category in most reporting.

10. Exchange rate is for January 1996: 1 ECU = $1.23.

11. Note that the three Baltic republics are included in Central and Eastern Europe, not the former Soviet Union, because this is the way they are treated in donor statistics.

12. The reviews consisted of structured interviews with the chief-of-party and reading of the formal statement of work for each project. Sketches of these projects are given in Annex B.

13. It is worth stressing that the cases have been selected to illustrate specific points. They are not a systematic sample of projects defined on some criterion so as to be representative in any sense. They were gathered opportunistically over seven years through reviewing documents, listening to presentations, participating in project reviews, and discussions with contractors, host country representatives, and senior aid officials. These sources were supplemented by the more purposeful analysis of a half-dozen projects in the Russian Federation and information provided by my Urban Institute colleagues on projects about which they have firsthand knowledge.

Chapter Two

WHAT IS SUCCESS?

Success, like beauty, may ultimately lie in the eye of the beholder. My purpose here, however, demands a more prosaic approach. I need a definition of success that is generally accepted and can be objectively measured and compared across projects. I begin the chapter by distilling such a definition from a range of previous efforts to define success in the technical cooperation arena. I then review the record of success in conducting technical cooperation projects in the former Soviet bloc. The record is not strong. This is, at least in part, because those working in the region—both donor officials and contractors executing the projects—tried to transfer directly their modes of implementing technical cooperation projects in other areas of the globe. To emphasize the perils of such an approach, I end the chapter by contrasting the environment facing technical cooperation in this region with the environment facing similar programs in less developed areas of the world.

DEFINING AND MEASURING SUCCESS

In a recent evaluation of ten USAID projects in Russia, the GAO employed two broad standards of measurement. The first is whether the project is fulfilling its stated objectives. The second is whether it is "contributing significantly to systemic reform" (GAO 1995a: 3). The GAO understood that the projects were only components of larger sector reform programs. But it argued, nevertheless, that all projects, and especially those with a large share of the aid budget for sector reform, should be judged on their contribution to the sustainability of structural reform.

The distinction between immediate, concrete outcomes and more slowly emerging and harder to measure effects is a common theme in the literature. In *Does Aid Work?*, for example, Robert Cassen divides the effects of technical cooperation projects into "the proximate and the ultimate" (Cassen 1994: 143–144). Proximate effects occur shortly after implementation and are usually quantifiable: number of officials trained, number of laws passed, number of demonstration projects initiated. Ultimate effects occur much later. They are not only harder to quantify, but also more difficult to trace back to a particular project. A project may have accomplished its stated objectives—had its proximate effects—without ever having the ultimate intended effects. Much more of the responsibility for the ultimate effects lies with the recipient country and the results depend upon how that recipient uses the technical cooperation experience.

The World Bank's *Handbook on Technical Assistance* (1993: 15) distinguishes between outputs and outcomes along similar lines. "Performance of the project's outputs can be evaluated in a relatively straightforward manner using data collected from the project. Outcomes, however, require a longer time frame, and they are often indirect, thus more difficult to assess." The OECD's Development Assistance Committee places the emphasis even more strongly on the long term. In *Principles for New Orientations in Technical Co-operation*, the first principle is to "set as strategic objectives of Technical Co-operation long-term capacity building in developing countries rather than immediate short-term performance improvement" (DAC/OECD 1991: 5).

One might consider the GAO's first criterion of success—to meet the stated objectives—as really an indicator of whether the second and main criterion of success is likely to be achieved—to strengthen, restructure, and improve institutions as they are broadly defined. In this context institutions extend beyond government agencies and "comprise both formal and informal rules and procedures" that govern the behavior of participants in social and economic transactions in a given sector (Schiavo-Campo 1994: 4). The proximate effects of a technical cooperation program are usually changing the formal rules of an institution. Formal rules can be changed by fiat. Informal rules and procedures can be changed only through time and attitude shifts.

To illustrate the time frame surrounding the different stages and effects of a technical cooperation program, consider the example of a program with the objective to encourage public participation in environmental policy-making.

In the first stage, the foreign advisors may work with the central government and the environmental ministry on drafting a new law or amending the country's national environmental act. To do this they would build relationships with key figures, raise awareness of the issue, and help draft the legislation. This process typically encompasses three months to a year. Within one to three years, the program might have several projects with different objectives, all of which would contribute to the program's ultimate goal. The projects might encompass creating a database of public information, training government officials in providing the public with information, working with NGOs on techniques to obtain and analyze information, and ensuring that public participation language is included in enabling legislation, regulatory procedures, and local laws.

This multi-faceted second stage is critical for sustainability. In our example, the intended ultimate effect of this array of projects is that environmental public participation in policy-making will be institutionalized both formally and informally. This means that officials in the relevant organizations must change their attitudes and behavior towards private individuals. It means that NGOs must build independence from both their government and international assistance and have the skills to serve as a watchdog of environmental policy-making and, more generally, democracy. It means that a considerable share of citizens are made aware of the government's policies, the effect on their lives, and the recourse available to them. The minimum time frame for these ultimate effects is probably three to five years.[1]

In addition to the two broad criteria of success formulated by the GAO, a third criterion is crucial—the extent to which the technical cooperation meets the needs of the recipient. This, in turn, is closely tied to recipient participation. In a report to the U.S. Congress, Janine Wedel describes how, early on, officials in Central and Eastern Europe felt frustration and resentment because the reality of assistance programs did not match their expectations. With time and experience this feeling diminished as recipients became "better at identifying their needs and more selective about foreign (and local) advisers" (Wedel 1994: 306).[2] In the early days of technical cooperation programs recipients may well have been in a poor position to define success since the process itself was not well understood. Sophistication has increased and in many instances host country officials are now fully capable of participating in the design process. This participation is crucial to ensure that the donor, the implementing organization, *and* the recipient have the same objectives. If their objectives are divergent, sustainable success will be elusive (Lethem and Cooper 1983: 6, 27).

It is useful to compare the three definitions of success I have introduced so far with the OECD's very comprehensive guidelines for determining program success. These state that an evaluation should examine the program, "with the aim of determining its efficiency, effectiveness, impact, sustainability and the relevance of the objectives."

Efficiency has no counterpart in the GAO schema, so I shall discuss it last. The OECD considers a program effective if it fulfills its stated objectives. This is very similar to the GAO's first (simple) criterion for program success. The OECD uses impact to refer to the "effect [of an aid intervention] on its surroundings in terms of technical, economic, socio-cultural, institutional and environmental factors," and sustainability to refer to "the extent to which the objectives of an activity will continue (to be reached) after the project assistance is over" (Berlage and Stokke 1992: 5). Together these two OECD criteria correlate well with the GAO's estimate of whether a program is "contributing significantly to systemic reform."

The OECD defines the relevance of a program's objectives in a way that parallels Wedel's and Lethem and Cooper's criterion that technical cooperation meet the needs of the recipient. As Wedel argues, "The problem is that the evaluations often fail to take into account local perceptions, realities, and responses" (Wedel 1994: 333). Programs do not exist in a vacuum; therefore, the context should be carefully considered before and during implementation.[3]

I now come to efficiency. To the OECD, a program is efficient if "it uses the least costly resources necessary to achieve its objectives" (Berlage and Stokke 1992: 5). Technical cooperation programs, as all other government expenditures, should be evaluated using the principles and procedures of economics and accounting. Two monetary approaches to evaluating public goods are cost-benefit analysis and cost-effectiveness analysis. The first approach requires a more exact definition of a program's benefits, since costs and benefits must be estimated and compared. Such analysis to evaluate technical cooperation programs has fallen in popularity in recent years, in part because economists "overestimated the availability of reliable project-level and economy-wide data" (Renard and Berlage 1992: 53).

Cost-effectiveness analysis takes as a given that a particular goal should be achieved and examines the costs of alternative means of achieving that goal. This does not mean that benefits should not be identified and measured, but it does avoid the often unsolvable problem of assigning a dollar value for each benefit. It is, thus, a useful tool for analyzing whether the same objectives could have been realized at a lower cost (Berlage and Stokke 1992: 19).

For the big picture, using the principles of cost-effectiveness almost always makes more sense than cost-benefit analysis. For example, the U.S. Congress has decided—for geopolitical, humanitarian, and economic reasons—that granting assistance to Eastern Europe and the NIS is worthy of taxpayer money. According to *Assistance to the Newly Independent States: A Status Report* (February 1994), the U.S. is "to operate programs with goals that include privatization, the creation of new markets for U.S. goods, democratization, and the transition from a defense-oriented to a civilian-based economy." Having established these goals, the U.S. government still has the responsibility to select programs that will achieve these goals in the most cost-effective manner. This implies that projects within each program should be held to a cost-effectiveness test, and that the programs should be compared with one another on the same basis.

The discussion so far leads me to propose the following principles for defining success in the technical cooperation context. To be successful, a program must meet its stated objectives, contribute to systemic reform, be sustainable and cost-effective, and meet the recipients' needs.

How in practice are technical cooperation programs evaluated? The literature suggests that an evaluation of a technical cooperation program should distinguish, and evaluate separately, the following three program components:

1. design and preparation
2. implementation and institutionalization
3. monitoring and evaluation.[4]

At the first level, a program should be judged on whether its short-term and long-term objectives were clearly outlined and whether they were developed together with the recipient, or at a minimum approved by the recipient. Did the implementing agency make the appropriate contacts within not only the sectoral ministry, but also the central ministries? Were distortions in institutions well understood? Was the absence of institutions identified? Were projects designed with a realistic aim at improving efficiency, effectiveness, or equity in the sector's functioning?

At the second level, the program should be judged on the implementation process of its projects, including dissemination of new ideas and practices in the country. Successful implementation will have a strong institutionalization element.

At the third level, the program should be judged on how it monitored its own progress as well as changes in the sector it was trying to reform, and how it made adjustments in strategy and tactics accordingly. In evaluating development projects Hirschman found that "the very ability of the project management to adjust to a changing environment is the main indicator of its success" (Berlage and Stokke 1992: 11). Not only are all countries not the same, but in transitional countries especially, the conditions that were true one month are not necessarily true the next.

The evaluation criteria just listed should be used for ongoing program management, not just ex post evaluations of success or failure. In the words of Lethem and Cooper (1983: 13),

> Because the state of the art in institutional TA is unclear and behavioral changes are often required in its implementation, this type of assistance should not be managed according to a 'blueprint,' but should be treated as an iterative process and probably broken down into discrete phases that take advantage of feedback, learning from experience, and appreciation of changes in the economic, political, or managerial context.

A program that makes a practice of evaluating itself and learning from its experiences will be able to respond to the changing needs of the recipient and lay the groundwork for systemic and sustainable reform. Unfortunately, as we shall see, most technical cooperation project managers focus strongly on the concrete, often narrow, objectives set forth in their contracts. Accomplishment of broader sector reform goals are frequently viewed as not part of the Terms of Reference.

THE RECORD[5]

Any summary judgment about the effectiveness of technical cooperation programs overall, not mentioning those explicitly in support of sector reform, is bedeviled by a paucity of rigorous evaluations and use of differing criteria among those who have conducted the evaluations available.

A review of evaluations that have been performed by USAID's Regional Inspector General, the U.S. Congress's General Accounting Office, and by independent contractors shows that while many of the U.S. government-supported technical cooperation projects achieved a majority of the stated goals, few projects could claim that they had made any significant contribution to systemic change.

According to a mid-course evaluation of privatization programs in Central and Eastern Europe, fewer than half of the firm-specific privatization projects were successful. The objectives of these types of projects were two: to help identify likely privatization candidates and to assist in their privatization. In most cases, however, the selection of candidates was random. More often than not, the project did not result in privatizing the selected enterprises and when privatization did occur, it was a lengthy and costly process.[6] A GAO review of the Russian commercial real estate project, for example, determined that it failed to meet its primary objective of replicating a pilot program in five other cities. The program managers decided to employ a different approach in each city, which both negated the purpose of the pilot program and failed to achieve the desired changes in any of the five cities.[7] An audit of a Department of Treasury program in Bulgaria found that little progress had been made on the project for creating a bank training facility. After almost a year since the arrival of the foreign advisor, he was performing only one of the five proposed activities and the training materials and computer equipment had not been delivered to the client.[8]

Projects failed to contribute to systemic change often because they were too narrow in scope or did not include components for reinforcing their progress. An example of a project that is too limited to have a sectoral effect is the NIS agribusiness partnership project. This project created six partnerships in the NIS, although there are 27,000 state and collective farms and 270,000 private farms in Russia alone.[9] A two-city scope for the Russian district heating project is likewise too small to be contributing to systemic reform. Indeed, even within the two the activities do not constitute systemic reform because they do not address energy efficiency policies.[10] Another example is a health care training project based on Russian policy initiatives that were subsequently dropped from the political agenda. Even without the change in political priorities, it was unrealistic to achieve an impact on Russia's health care sector and democratic free-market system through a two-week training course.[11] A final example is training provided by a Department of Labor project in Poland. The program had potential for creating entrepreneurs, but "lacked some key linkages in such areas as helping graduates obtain start-up business financing and providing follow-up technical assistance to graduates who started their own businesses."[12] Unless training programs are part of a larger reform strategy for the sector, they rarely have a significant impact on sectoral reform.

If forced to give my *impression* of the overall success rates to date, based on the available record, my scoring would align with the findings of the GAO in its 1995 evaluation of ten USAID projects in Russia. In terms of meeting the objectives defined for the project, 20 percent met or exceeded them, 50 percent met some but not all, and 30 percent were failures, i.e., met few or none. In terms of contributing to systemic and sustainable reform, 30 percent of the projects received a passing grade.[13]

More instructive than the overall scoreboard, however, are the problems and strengths identified in the project evaluations, since these can be the basis for taking steps to increase the odds of success.

PROBLEMS

The evaluations revealed several serious problems in technical cooperation projects in Central and Eastern Europe and the NIS that occur with some regularity. These are slow start-up, weak partnerships with clients, little monitoring or evaluation, and poor dissemination and replication of results.

Slow Start-Up. When evaluators identified a slow start to the program as a problem, they often noted that it had serious repercussions through the life of the program. There are several examples from a 1993 independent contractor evaluation of USAID privatization programs in the Czech Republic, Hungary, and Poland. In at least one case in the Czech Republic program delay caused the "Government [to] lose interest in the concept [which] has therefore changed the scope of the project."[14] The pilot privatization project of a state farm in Hungary accomplished very little because of a change in the local political climate. The evaluators argue that if more progress was made earlier, "privatization might have gotten through before the climate changed."[15] In Poland, in particular, it was late (U.S.) authorization of privatization projects that "undermined credibility generally and probably contributed to the negative attitude present in some quarters."[16]

Another reason for slow start-up is difficulty in placing qualified staff in the country. A GAO review of the environmental policy and technology project in Russia identified at least four cases where critical staff arrived four to six months after the positions were funded. This set back work since the complex project involving many local players could not be managed adequately from Washington.[17] After the qualified staff are located, it still takes time to educate them about local conditions. For example, a privatization project for nonferrous metal companies in the Czech Republic had a slow start-up because of the time needed for the "contractor to become familiar with the industry."[18] Even the otherwise successful privatization project with the Czech Savings Bank suffered from a slow start-up for similar reasons.[19]

Delay also eats into the time available for project implementation. In a training program to support democracy in Poland delay and poor organization left "too little time for clarifying translations and developing Polish examples," which severely undercut the training's effectiveness.[20]

Weak Partnerships. Delivering technical cooperation assumes that at least two parties are involved, but often the aid providers fail to identify a client, select the wrong one, or have poor client relations. The University of South Carolina program to "foster decentralization and strengthen local government in Bulgaria" first decided to work in the country's three largest cities. When it became apparent that those cities did not have a supportive political and legal climate, the program managers responded by redirecting the focus to six smaller and more appropriate cities.[21] This early recognition of the problem did not occur with the Russian commercial real estate project, however. The program managers attempted unsuccessfully to replicate the pilot program in five cities where the relevant local officials did not support the program goals in any case.[22] The Russian health care training project provided training that the beneficiaries found useful, but the beneficiaries "lacked the authority, expertise, or resources to influence reforms." Such influence was the program goal.[23]

Sometimes the correct client is identified, but the relationship between provider and client is weak, because the client was not adequately consulted in the design and preparation stage of the project. For example, while the program managers of the environmental policy and technology project in Russia consulted the Ministry of Environmental Protection and Natural Resources in selecting project cities, they did not involve the ministry in designing the project. This weak partnership "reduced the likelihood the project could be duplicated on a wider scale."[24] Likewise, a Department of Treasury project in Bulgaria aimed at creating a sustainable bank training facility, but lacked a formal agreement with the local implementing institute. When the agreement could not be reached, the client not only refused to provide the American advisor with the promised housing and office space, but continually rejected his advice and assistance.[25]

Lack of Monitoring and Evaluation. Monitoring has a role irrespective of the size or type of technical cooperation project. Yet, according to the program evaluations, very few programs address this systematically. When technical cooperation is combined with a capital investment, it is often treated as an event, rather than a process. For example, the district heating project in Russia failed to monitor whether the equipment was actually installed or measure its impact on energy savings.[26] The industrial energy component of the emergency energy project in CEE was similarly guilty. According to the program evaluators the lack of follow-up meant that "the monitoring and measuring equipment left in the host countries at the conclusion of the EEP has been underutilized."[27]

Monitoring and evaluation are also often lacking in training programs. An assessment of the privatization training programs in Central and Eastern Europe showed that they had little targeting, no formal plans, and no monitoring and evaluation, except for one project in Hungary.[28] The Department of Commerce's internship programs for NIS business managers failed to give interns input into their training plans, contact and monitor them during the internships, or conduct exit interviews. This explains why half of the participants interviewed by the auditors reported that the training received in the United States could not be applied to their work.[29]

Poor Dissemination and Replication of Results. A majority of the evaluations cited inadequate dissemination as a problem. The environmental training program in CEE was praised for innovative training techniques, but criticized for producing only one "quarterly" newsletter within a 2.5-year period.[30] The evaluation of firm-specific privatization projects in CEE found a case "where a final report was rendered to the subject company only in English."[31]

Since dissemination can greatly increase the impact of a program, evaluators are understandably critical when it is ignored in otherwise good programs. The evaluators of the World Environment Center project for providing industrial audits commented that "the impact on visited plants and the multiplier effect might have been substantially greater if WEC had a system in place to follow-up, monitor, analyze and disseminate the results of those visits."[32] One of the lessons learned from the industrial energy component of the emergency energy project was that transfer of information requires "a well-directed effort" and does not happen automatically, as assumed by the program managers.[33]

Few projects have laid the groundwork for achieving similar results from demonstration programs throughout the country. For example, the Department of Labor program set up model employment offices in Bulgaria, but lacked a plan for how they would be replicated across the country. While highly skilled employees did facilitate the replication process, it was wrong to assume that this would substitute for an organization plan.[34] The firm-specific privatization projects in

Central and Eastern Europe may have been envisioned as demonstration projects of a kind, but the program evaluators point out that the results relate to one firm only and efforts cannot be replicated. This makes firm-specific privatization projects less cost-effective than projects to assist facilitating institutions that can have a broader impact.[35]

HIGHLIGHTS FROM GOOD PROJECTS

The foregoing catalogue of ineptitude is balanced by numerous examples of projects with positive attributes identified by the same evaluation teams.

While training components of some programs are treated as an activity of little real value, the Environmental Training Program demonstrates that training can serve as a catalyst to systemic reform. The program operated in six countries in the region and the evaluation covered activities in Poland, Bulgaria, and Romania. To begin with, the program designers had realistic goals for their limited resources and decided to concentrate efforts on priority regions within each country. Then they sought out the appropriate partners. According to the authors of the program's mid-course evaluation, the In-Country Coordinators "have shown remarkable initiative and imagination in mobilizing local partners among NGOs, local/regional government units, training institutes and businesses, to support, implement and extend program results."[36] In the training workshops these diverse groups learned to negotiate and approach problems in a pragmatic and systematic fashion. Today, indigenous organizations are tackling and "producing concrete remedies for ecological problems that two years ago were seen as intractable, hopeless disasters."[37] The program is achieving sustainability because program managers understood where their local counterparts would be willing to invest their efforts and funds once U.S. participation ended.

The housing and urban sector program in Central and Eastern Europe was commended for, among other things, flexibility in seeking clients and creating promising pilot programs.[38] When administrative and political troubles held back reform in the capital cities, the program managers responded to "policy reform" clients with initiatives in other cities.[39] These clients gave the necessary support for developing local pilot programs that now command attention at the national level. As I have already noted, pilot programs are able to demonstrate the effectiveness of reform when pure theory fails to convince national leaders. Appreciating the value of a successful local project, the program managers devised a well-thought-out and varied set of activities that would reinforce one another. Both the housing finance reform project in Poland and the rent/housing allowance project in Hungary involved a "comprehensive sequencing of policy reform, institution reform, technical assistance and training."[40] While noting these successes, the evaluators mention that early programs were uneven and slow, because the advisors were instructed to respond to the needs of the recipient governments even though the latter did not have the ability to articulate these. This problem was remedied by greater field presence so advisors could work closely with the governments on creating country-specific strategy statements that now drive the program development process.[41]

In 1992 the USAID privatization program in the Czech Republic achieved success when it "shifted away from assisting individual firms, to focusing more on assisting institutions and targeted transactional assistance."[42] Although privatization eventually releases the government of duties, implementing a privatization program requires an adept governmental agency. Crimson Capital/Deloitte & Touche was established to assist the Czech Ministry of Privatization in privatization transactions, particularly with foreign investors. During periods of rapid staff changeover, Crimson Capital provided "credibility and consistency" for the Czech privatization program; in return it enjoyed the strong support of the Ministry of Privatization. By mid-March 1993, Crimson Capital had facilitated the privatization of 63 enterprises with 40 more expected in the near future. While the expertise contributed by Deloitte & Touche was critical, the project recognized that a local company can be more effective when it comes to politically charged issues. Indeed, by creating a local institution to pave the way for foreign investment in the Czech Republic, the project might have helped prevent the type of backlash against foreign investment that did happen in neighboring Hungary.[43]

The training-of-trainers program in Poland developed an indigenous and sustainable capacity to train local government officials by selecting a local partner with experience and an established network. Under the direction of the (Polish) Foundation in Support of Local Democracy (FSLD), regional centers provide training in local government, management, and financing. "Between January 1–June 15, 1994 FSLD conducted 530 training courses attended by 11,611 individuals." Although FSLD accepts funding from various sources, the centers charge fees for their courses, which cover most of the related costs. Other indications of its sustainability are the high retention of trainers and the "demand-driven" programs and field initiatives. The payoffs of identifying and supporting such organizations are great, which serves as a reminder of potential local capacity.[44]

The Environmental Law Institute (ELI) carried out the legal activities component of the Cooperative Agreement between USAID and the World Environmental Center for the Central and Eastern Europe program. According to an independent evaluation of the program, ELI contributed significantly to new environmental legislation in the countries of the region and established ongoing linkages with environmental lawyers, NGO activists, academics and government officials. Their "on-site and hands-on" approach allowed ELI to provide drafts, revisions, and testimony as needed by the governmental bodies. "ELI's responses to requests for information or assistance have been timely, flexible to changing conditions and, from the standpoint of their primary clients, wholly satisfactory."[45] In addition, the ELI team demonstrated their expertise by and received much feedback from translating and distributing working papers that introduced new concepts to ministries, universities, and local authorities. This dual approach to policy change is instructive: The theories behind the new concepts were disseminated widely in an accessible fashion, while their application to the particular country was ironed out through team negotiations with local participants.[46]

WHAT IS DIFFERENT ABOUT THE FORMER SOVIET BLOC

One of the common assumptions in the early days of the transition about providing sector technical cooperation to the countries of Eastern Europe and the NIS was that the lessons learned so laboriously in developing countries about carrying out such projects would form a solid basis for the new work. For reasons outlined below, only a limited degree of transfer turned out to be possible.

The most fundamental difference between working in the countries of the former Soviet bloc and developing nations, especially in the early years of transition, was motivation and the desire for change. In the words of Scott Thomas (1995: 2):

> What had been learned from the experience of working for decades in developing countries was that frequently the principal barrier to implementation of sound economic policies were politicians and bureaucrats and businessmen who had what was politely called "access" to them—*nomenklatura*, if you will—who benefitted from the political regime as it was. . . . In contrast, in Eastern Europe following the "Velvet Revolution," American aid officials faced what was as close as one could hope to come to the complete convergence of the two objectives—further-

ance of American foreign policy and host-country economic reform objectives—because, after all, it was the Communist *nomenklatura* that
has so miserably failed in the conduct of economic policy, and our mission was to advise and assist their successors.

In short, change was actively sought. Willing clients were readily
available.[47] The speed of reform put a special premium on rapid mo-
bilization of donor support, hence the attention to start-up problems
in the project evaluations.

The pressure for change brings to light a second basic difference
between operations in the two groups of countries: the extent of legislative change required. Many sector technical cooperation projects
in Asia, Africa, and Latin America require little in the way of legislative change, although adjustments to program regulations are often
necessary. The contrast with the countries in the former Soviet bloc
is stark. Some of these countries began the transition for the replacement of their entire legal system with a rule-of-law system. A new
constitution and civil code were top priorities. For others the pre-
socialist property law framework has been left in place and it has
been more a task of stripping away accretions than starting from
scratch. National-level laws to restructure each sector were typically
necessary for both groups of countries.[48] Corresponding requirements
for technical cooperation projects followed: Teams had to be heavy on
policy design and legal expertise as well as the more typical capabilities in institutional reform and strengthening. The "policy experts"
needed to have a solid understanding of the Soviet planned economy
model so that they knew not only where a sector was coming from
but also its western-oriented destination.

Three other cardinal differences between the countries of the former
Soviet bloc and developing countries as clients for sector technical
cooperation projects should be kept in mind. First, the level of basic
education of the professional class was high and a true *intelligentsia*
of substantial size already existed. The basic abilities of officials,
institute researchers, and managers meant that new ideas were absorbed relatively quickly. Second, a competent, if not client-oriented,
administrative structure was in place. The combination of these two
factors meant that recipients of technical cooperation projects could
be assigned some of the burden of developing new policies and procedures and implementing them. The more they did themselves, the more
committed to reforms they would be. In these circumstances, advisors
can be more "idea people" than drafters of detailed regulations.

Finally, the countries had well-developed social and physical infrastructure. True, the physical infrastructure was not close to western

standards, but it was certainly higher than in developing countries. Again, this altered the tasks faced by the donor and the country. The emphasis in the short run could be on using the existing infrastructure more efficiently rather than creating it.

In short, the facile, if implicit, assumption of donors and consultants of strong similarities between developing nations and the countries of the former Soviet bloc in the tasks to be done and the mode of execution in sector technical assistance projects proved way off the mark. The tasks are very different—a lesson that has now been learned by the donors and their agents but at considerable cost.

This is not to say that the tasks *within* the area are uniform. Variation in conditions is considerable, and needs to be taken into account in designing technical cooperation programs. The high standard of living and affinity for reform in Hungary and the Czech Republic, during the transition for example, contrast starkly with the situation in Belarus in 1996. Similarly, the comparatively low level of development in Albania and the Kyrgyz Republic demand different priorities for technical cooperation and different approaches.[49] The lessons I recount in later chapters are better suited for technical cooperation work in the more economically advanced countries.

The question addressed in the balance of this book is how to improve on the spotty record of technical cooperation projects in the former Soviet bloc, especially those aimed at sector reform. The next five chapters shift the perspective from searching for problems to defining practices important for project success. They also provide a comprehensive analysis of the workings of sector reform technical cooperation projects.

Notes

1. Mosley argues that the "effectiveness of any operation is the extent to which it is able to sustain itself after external aid money is withdrawn." Therefore, he proposes that a "significant proportion (at least 25 percent) of all the TC evaluations of any aid agency should be conducted three years or more after the termination of the operation." (Mosley 1992: 81)

2. Wedel also makes the case that ignoring the recipient's opinions and concerns will surely have negative effects on the program. She maintains that "recipients in key positions can frustrate or encourage the implementation of consultants' recommendations. They can direct aid to their friends or encourage aid to be used to benefit a wider public." (Wedel 1994: 333)

3. As noted by Berlage and Stokke (1992: 8), "To be effective, aims have to be operationalized and adapted to a variety of social, cultural, economic and political environments; efforts to this end have nowhere been particularly strong or persistent."

4. In the 1970s, USAID developed a system called the Logical Framework Analysis, which has been more recently adapted and adopted by most European countries. According to the Logical Framework Analysis,

> The specific objectives of a project are to be clarified at the design stage; the planners should identify project inputs, outputs, purposes and goals (intermediate objectives and the ultimate impact), along with objectively verifiable indicators of progress in attaining these objectives, hypotheses about causal linkages and assumptions about the conditions in the project environments on which these were based (Berlage and Stokke 1992: 28).

By requiring that indicators of success be incorporated into the project design, evaluators can better compare the intended and actual effects. Armed with indicators, evaluators then need to assess each program component or stage to determine when and how hypotheses and assumptions broke down and when they proved to be true. According to the OECD guidelines, an evaluation should consist of an examination of "an ongoing or completed project or programme, its design, implementation and results." (Berlage and Stokke 1992: 5). In analyzing the success of World Bank technical cooperation projects, Lethem and Cooper (1983: 13, 20) similarly use identification, design and implementation as the focus for examination.

5. The documents reviewed in preparing this section are listed in Annex D.

6. Development Economics Group/Louis Berger International and Checchi and Company 1993: ii, 131–133.

7. GAO 1995a: 56.

8. Regional Inspector General [RIG] 1994: 6–9.

9. GAO 1995a: 58.

10. Ibid., p. 47.

11. GAO 1995a: 49–52.

12. RIG 1993c: ii.

13. An internal World Bank (1996b: 25) evaluation report, looking at overall experience with its project portfolio, judged that one in three of its operations in 1994 had not made an acceptable contribution to development and that the percentage of satisfactory outcomes was too low to be acceptable.

14. Development Economics Group/Louis Berger International and Checchi and Company 1993: 145.

15. Ibid., p. 177.

16. Ibid., p. 37.

17. GAO 1995a: 42–43.

18. Development Economics Group/Louis Berger International and Checchi and Company 1993: 140.

19. Ibid., p. 143.

20. Foster, Grossman, and Young 1994: 9.

21. Foster, Grossman, and Young 1994: 6.

22. GAO 1995a: 57.

23. Ibid., p. 52.

24. GAO 1995a: 43.

25. RIG 1994: 6–9.

26. GAO 1995a: 47.

27. Scientech 1994: 15.

28. Development Economics Group/Louis Berger International and Checchi and Company 1993: 41.

29. RIG 1993b: 9–10.

30. Hobgood, Muller, and Van Orsdol 1995: 19.

31. Development Economics Group/Louis Berger International and Checchi and Company 1993: 37.

32. Baser and Holmes 1992: 11.

33. Scientech 1994: 49.

34. RIG 1993a: 9.

35. Development Economics Group/Louis Berger International and Checchi and Company 1993: 33.

36. Hobgood, Muller, and Orsdol 1995: 2.

37. Ibid., p. 2.

38. Merrill, Phipps, Garnett, and Maxian 1993: 2–3.

39. Ibid., p. 12.

40. Ibid., p. 18.

41. Ibid., pp. 3, 7.

42. Development Economics Group/Louis Berger International and Checchi and Company 1993: 53.

43. Ibid., pp. 26–28, 53, 133–136.

44. Foster, Grossman, and Young 1994: Appendix B, pp. 6–15.

45. Baser and Holmes 1992: 27.

46. Ibid., pp. 23–27.

47. Of course, after the initial "honeymoon with the market," more normal political competition reappeared and the pace of reform slowed.

48. See Rapaczynski (1996) and World Bank (1996a, Chapter 5) for an overview of areas of legal reform to support the development of market relations.

49. According to the World Bank's *1996 World Development Report*, Albania and the Kyrgyz Republic were officially classified as "low income economies." Albania's 1994 per capita GDP was about the same as those of the Central African Republic and Ghana. The level in the Kyrgyz Republic was about the same as in Sri Lanka. In contrast, the Czech Republic, Hungary, and Slovenia are classed with nations such as Brazil, Mexico, and South Korea.

Part Two

ENTRANCE STRATEGY

Chapter Three

DEFINING THE PROJECT

Our story begins just after the donor agency has decided to invest in a technical cooperation program in a particular sector in one of the nations of the former Soviet bloc. A sector can be selected for many reasons and through processes of varying sophistication. Selection may result from the importance of the sector to the recipient nation's overall economic performance: oil exploitation in oil producing nations and improved efficiency of the rail system being examples. Alternatively, the donor may be responding to a clear priority request from the host country. Selection may also be driven from the supply side. A donor, for example, may decide to specialize throughout the region in a certain sector (health care or banking reform, for instance). Restructuring the chosen sector may not be the highest priority for a particular country at a specific moment. Improvement is necessary at some time, and a multi-country program will be much more efficiently implemented than a more piecemeal approach. Less altruistically, a bilateral donor may decide to field a program to help promote business opportunities for the donor country.

The process of sector selection is similarly wide ranging. Perhaps the simplest process is a direct decision by a high official based primarily on domestic business considerations. At the most complex end of the spectrum, the donor's staff could invest substantial time and money in assessing the relative payoff of technical cooperation projects in various sectors. Such assessments require analytical studies, which usually entail fresh data gathering and other field work. Only a tentative decision will usually be made before checking on the extent to which other donors are currently working or planning to work in the sector and having the proposal for the project vetted by the host government.

The basic decision to develop a technical cooperation project in a particular sector is not typically informed by a detailed project design proposal, unless it is part of the implementation of a capital project, such as a World Bank loan. Indeed, what might be done is often very sketchy at this stage. Following a tentative decision to work in a sector, the first step must be to define the project, which includes a more careful analysis of its feasibility. Several options exist for developing the program design (called the identification mission), all involving significant work in the recipient country.

For those exceptional donor countries and multilateral donors that have a resident aid mission in the recipient country with the requisite technical skills, the local staff can be assigned the task of developing the project. Often the limited local staff will be supplemented by expatriate consultants. The more common arrangement, however, is for experts to be dispatched to the country for this purpose. Multilateral donors typically favor using their own staff; bilateral donors typically rely more heavily on consultants. Donor staff have the advantage of knowledge of the donor's requirements and procedures. Consultants usually bring greater sector expertise to the mission.

FEASIBILITY

These definition missions must address two types of feasibility questions. The first is whether the knowledge exists to address the particular problem defined as central to reform. In principle, applied research may be needed to develop a deeper knowledge base before launching a comprehensive sector reform project.[1] In fact, many projects failed this feasibility test in the early years of donor sector technical cooperation projects in Eastern Europe and the NIS. The knowledge base was thin and the true experts extremely rare. In practice this test was frequently waived because of the urgency of proceeding and the realization that learning-by-doing rather than studies would likely be a more productive method for acquiring knowledge. Today, the test should be applied quite rigorously.

The second feasibility hurdle is developing a partnership with the recipient government, or at least its compliance for going forward with the project.[2] In fact, agreements are reached at various levels. At the broadest level, the donor and the recipient country sign an agreement on technical cooperation and other forms of aid. Usually this gives the donor wide latitude in the issues that might be addressed. The U.S.-Russian Federation agreement is of this form, for example. At the next level, the donor and host country government may sign an agreement about a particular project. Finally, if the donor will be working with provincial or local governments as part of its project, agreements are likely to be signed with them as well.

CASE: In the course of March 1992, the HSRP negotiated agreements with the Russian Federation and three local governments. At the Federation level the team was careful to have the agreement signed by three agencies: the Ministry of Construction, the Ministry of Economy, and the Economic Reform Working Center, a new organization set up Yegor Gaidar to push reform. The Ministry of Construction had nominal responsibility for the housing sector, but the team feared that its lack of responsibility for finance policy might prevent the team from receiving cooperation from government agencies in its planned work on housing finance issues. The breadth of the responsibilities assigned to the three agencies signing the agreement guaranteed that the team could work unimpeded.

CASE: In another project, in contrast, the decision was made to avoid working with the conservative Ministry of Health in a USAID health sector reform project in Russia. This was a donor-initiated project. According to the project managers, the idea was to work directly with reform-minded provincial governments, while keeping the central ministry informed. In any event, the contract for technical cooperation was signed with a U.S. firm without a Russian central government sponsor in place. The result was that the project was substantially blocked in its early phase by the lack of ministry concurrence: provincial governments looked to Moscow for approval. Under 1991 legislation provincial health officials have the legal right to decide to participate without ministry approval, but they proved reluctant to do so.

Signing these agreements is important for removing roadblocks, but should not be expected to guarantee enthusiastic support from the local signatories. In addition to removing barriers to implementation, agreements with host governments should be viewed as an opportunity to set a concrete agenda. In the early years of reform in the region, few host country officials understood what was meant by technical cooperation programs. Their unfamiliarity with the process made them poor partners in designing projects. Merrill et al. criticized some early USAID projects in this area; citing the inappropriateness of a program design that relied on officials in the recipient countries to articulate the types of technical assistance needed (officials who often displayed a lack of knowledge about market systems and what was needed to implement them) (Merrill et al. 1993).

The situation has definitely improved but it is still spotty. Very often the donor, either the official from the donor agent or a consultant acting as his agent, has tentatively defined the project, or at least the limits of the project, and is vetting the idea with officials for acceptability. But simply asking an official what type of assistance his agency could use, besides additional funding, produces answers that tend to focus on a short-term problem immediately needing attention or on a very broad agenda that is beyond the resources of the donor or impractical at any resource level. Such discussions are not very satisfactory to either side.

Lesson: Use a "menu" approach to guide the discussion between the donor and local officials. This should be an annotated list of areas on which the project is prepared to work, which should be translated for distribution to meeting participants.

CASE: The HSRP used the "menu" approach successfully with both Russian Federation and local government officials. The list had been worked out in Washington with USAID officials in advance of the project definition mission to Russia. For instance, reform to eliminate rent controls and increase rents in the state housing sector was on the list, but restructuring the state construction firms (*kombinats*) was not.

The meetings followed a general pattern of the team explaining the nature of USAID's involvement in Russia generally and the broad scope of this specific project. The Russian officials would explain the challenges they faced in the sector, usually concentrating on the most acute. At this stage the team asked how the project might be of help in addressing their problems, making clear that no capital assistance was available. To focus the discussion the officials were handed the "menu" to consider. Without fail the review of the menu focused the remaining discussion. Usually the final phase was to obtain a priority ranking of the areas in which assistance would be most beneficial.

Meetings of this type were held with about a dozen officials at the Federation level and in each of the cities in which an assistance agreement was being negotiated. At the end of a full round of meetings, there was a quite clear consensus about priorities. It was then possible to hold a highly productive meeting with the mayor or deputy minister to report on the results of the previous discussions and to solicit his views as to whether he agreed with the priorities of his subordinates.[3]

The menu tends to anchor the discussion in the realm of what is realistic for technical cooperation projects to accomplish.

CASE: When a new phase of the HSRP program was launched under a second contract, the contract specified that the new work be in three substantive areas and concentrated in four cities. HSRP had been active in all four cities and the mayors of each were known to be reform-minded. While the topics of assistance had been discussed in general with Russian Federation officials, neither the mayors nor other officials had been consulted. The result was a tepid response by some of the cities, particularly Moscow, to the work program. Eventually a more demand-driven approach, broadening the services of the project to other cities, was adopted.

The European Union's PHARE and TACIS programs have relied heavily on host country agencies to define projects. In very general terms, the procedure is for the EU and the recipient government to decide on an "indicative program" at the sector level, including a broad allocation of the available resources among sectors. The sectors in which the EU will provide support are defined in advance.[4] A government aid coordination agency then compiles a list of requests for aid for each sector, including technical cooperation projects, from the relevant ministries and other agencies on an annual basis.[5] The list is rank-ordered to reflect the government's priorities. The EU program works from this list and the associated project descriptions; ultimately the list is approved by an EU management committee. In the Russian Federation, the TACIS program, in addition to the national program, has selected two regions each year with which to work and regional governments (*oblasts*) have compiled the project lists.

The procedure has the great virtue of being strongly recipient-driven. It can, however, produce a scatter-gun assistance program and militate against comprehensive sector reform projects since ministries tend to request discrete project assistance.

The tendency for recipient-driven work programs to be diffuse can, however, be controlled by the donor by establishing clear project areas in which it will work and permitting national or local governments to define specific projects within these.

CASE: Beginning in 1995 the Local Government Initiative (LGI) has been a major component of the USAID technical cooperation program in Bulgaria. The LGI includes association building, training, and demonstration projects in ten municipalities. Broadly, the program seeks to make municipalities more efficient and effective in the management of their resources and to make local governments more democratic, accountable, and responsive to their citizens.

USAID selected the ten municipalities for the demonstration program from among those with whom the agency had previously worked. The mayors were viewed as progressive and the local administrations as reasonably competent and responsive. At a kickoff meeting attended by the mayors and one or two key staff, each municipality defined five priority projects that were expected to benefit from external assistance and a small amount of grant funding. Over the following weeks the project director visited each of the municipalities to refine the list, clarify the contents of the priority projects, and begin developing an implementation plan.

The project team and USAID set only very broad limits on the types of projects that could be included and generally guided the selection process by describing types of projects that had been implemented successfully in Bulgaria or elsewhere in Eastern Europe. After the fifty projects had been defined (five for each municipality), the project team grouped them into categories to facilitate summary.

In the first 15 months of implementation the lack of focus within each city and among the municipalities proved a problem. The project had difficulty in fielding all of the required expertise and the cities lacked the absorption capacity to cope with so many diverse projects. As a result, project managers worked with the municipalities directly to redefine the work programs—and this time the process was guided by a list of categories into which projects would have to fall to be acceptable. The second round essentially employed the "menu" approach and produced a manageable work program.[6]

It should be emphasized that developing a good relationship with national-level ministries or the mayor's office at the local level does not preclude working with private sector entities. For example, the Housing Sector Reform Program works with commercial banks and with local housing maintenance firms with the loose cooperation of federal and local officials, respectively. It would be possible to work with both types of entities without any reference to government. However, obtaining the necessary legislative and regulatory changes would have been very difficult at best; and the project would have been at best marginally successful.

Lesson: Involve local technical experts as early as possible in the design process.

This sounds obvious but in fact is rarely done. Donor officials or consultants arrive in a country with introductions to government officials and possibly to other resident donor representatives and consultants implementing related projects. These contacts lead to others in the same circle. But there is no connection to the wider community of experts in the host country. This is vincible ignorance and can be addressed before the project definition team arrives in a country.

> CASE: The head of the Urban Institute team sent to define the HSRP consulted with Hungarian housing experts, whom he knew well, about who were the best professionals with whom he might work in Russia. They made a recommendation and supplied a phone number. The Russian expert was available to accept the assignment of working intensely for an initial one-week period and was ready to work on the day the team arrived in Moscow.

Many consultants have been conditioned by working with technically more limited local nationals in developing countries and therefore do not think naturally of involving local experts in the design process.

> CASE: A two-man team, both members new to Russia, from a U.S. consulting firm visited Moscow as part of its project identification mission. They met with the HSRP team, among others, to obtain information on developments in the housing sector. When it was suggested that the team could benefit from engaging a local consultant to help them understand the local situation better, the response from one consultant fresh from a long assignment in the Middle East was that they would hire Russians after the project was operational and an office established—the idea being that local professionals would be needed only for routine work.

> CASE: A USAID official sent out to define a municipal finance project which was to include Moscow as a demonstration site was directed to an official in the mayor's office as a suitable counterpart. In fact, the more suitable official was a deputy mayor responsible for the city's financial complex—a fact Russian experts would have known. When the contract was signed and the consultants began

work, it took them several months of frustrating work before shifting to the appropriate client.

Local experts bring several strengths to defining a project. First, they know how the current system works and they have a sense of which reforms are more likely to be accepted initially. They understand who stands to gain and lose from particular reforms and may be able to gauge the extent of resistance proposed reforms may provoke. Second, they know the organizational structure (formal and informal) of the national and local administrations: who in principle has more power and who must be involved in a particular decision if it is to be implemented in practice. Third, local consultants know the players—who is reform-oriented, who is not. Finally, in meetings they will understand vastly more of what is really being said than a donor official or consultant who must very often rely on translation. Translators give the basic message but they rarely understand enough about the context or subject to give the essential post-meeting debriefing.

BE REALISTIC, BE FLEXIBLE

There is a tendency for sector reform technical cooperation projects in Eastern Europe and the NIS to be defined with excessively ambitious objectives. This may have been encouraged by the initial sense of urgency in the first year or two of transition in each country and the underestimation of the task to be done. Overambitious objectives also result from terms of reference being developed by those who do not really understand the specific factors that will be involved in accomplishing the objectives—especially those parts that will be beyond the contractors' control, such as obtaining essential changes in laws or regulations. Competition within donor organizations for resources also contributes to "goal inflation."

A particular fault is in the length of time specified for a task.[7]

CASE: USAID, using its "omnibus contract" (which permits it to hold rapid competitions among prequalified firms) issued a task order for conducting pilot projects on reforming the land use regulation system of several municipalities. The contractor was to design a western-type land use regulatory system, help local officials draft the local ordinances necessary for the new system to be implemented, provide computer hardware and software for the new system, give substantial training to local officials, implement the new system in a couple of districts of each city, and establish a functioning zoning commission. The time specified for the work was eight months.[8] Most unrealistic in the terms of reference was failure to take explicit account of the time that could be required for local governments to pass the necessary legislation. Therefore, the time for the project was extended to give more adequate time for those tasks to be accomplished. At this writing the project is still ongoing.

The USAID Regional Inspector General documented this pattern of unrealistically compressed schedules in one of its reports and cited it as a weakness.[9] USAID managers responded that short work periods were deliberately used as a technique of controlling contractor performance, giving a clear opportunity to change contractors if necessary.

CASE: In mid-1996 the European Bank for Reconstruction and Development issued a one-year, $4 million contract for a competitively selected firm to work with a single, large Russian enterprise (as a demonstration) to restructure its operations with particular emphasis on inducing the enterprise to shed its "social assets" (i.e., housing, health clinics, day care facilities, and the like which the enterprise operated for the benefit of its employees). Among the tasks to be accomplished are selection of the enterprise from a group of candidates in five cities named by the contract manager; assisting with general restructuring efforts (including help with marketing, financial management, production planning, and creating an investment plan and identifying sources of investment); developing and implementing a plan for divestiture of the firm's social assets; and working with officials of the local government on restructuring the city's finances so as to be able to support the operation of the social assets divested to it. Additionally, the contractor was to prepare detailed manuals describing generic strategies for social asset restructuring based on the lessons learned in the pilot project.[10] While the overall level of effort may be reasonable, the one-year performance period seems highly questionable.

Project phasing is an important part of being realistic. There are good reasons for a project to begin with a modest level of effort and expand as it achieves success (discussed in detail in chapter 4). Early project implementation is necessarily spent learning the essential background about the sector, getting to know the current situation, refining the tasks to be done, recruiting local professional staff, and establishing an initial working relationship with local counterparts. A larger team only marginally reduces the time needed to accomplish this phase. The team leader must directly handle many of these tasks because he or she has to know the people and the substance.[11]

Lesson: Project designs that force-feed resources into the project start-up through overly ambitious time schedules are a mistake. Projects should start small and expand as additional resources can be effectively employed.

A tight statement of work is highly desirable, as the contractor then can develop a concrete proposal for doing the work with some certainty. At the same time, under the normal procurement rules conducting the competition takes six or more months unless donors have used some sort of competitive prequalification procedure that can shorten the process, like that noted in the above case involving USAID. In the countries of the former Soviet bloc changes in the policy environment that strongly affect the project can occur during preparation of the statement of work.

> CASE: The statement of work in the Request for Proposals for the second phase of the HSRP included working with enterprises and municipalities to streamline the process of transferring enterprise housing to the municipalities for operation. In general, getting enterprises out of the business of providing social services is viewed as important to increasing the overall efficiency of their operations (O'Leary et al. 1996). The Statement of Work called for the contractor to develop incentives to induce enterprises to give up their housing. In the nine months between when the project was defined and the contract was signed, enterprises in large numbers had decided that shedding their housing was rational and during this period enterprises began transferring several hundred thousand units per month to local governments. Thus, it was necessary at the very outset of the project to redefine the task as helping municipalities digest their new responsibilities, including encouraging the formation of condominium associations which would take complete responsibility and ownership for their buildings. Designing incentives to encourage divestiture was already irrelevant.

Projects are normally launched without a post-award examination of changes in conditions. The contractor usually discovers such changes during the first few months of work and shifts his work program accordingly. He will discuss the changes with the donor project officer and get his agreement on shifting the work program. But the changes seldom get reflected in the officially stated targets in the contract. This can lead to obvious problems when an external project review or evaluation is conducted. But a deeper problem is that it almost guarantees inefficient project start-up. If the changes in the sector during the competition have been great, the project may even select resident advisors with the wrong skills. It is clearly inefficient to have the contractor act initially on the basis of the terms of reference in the contract while learning only gradually that these operating premises are wrong.[12]

Lesson: Donor managers should reexamine the underlying premises of the project immediately after contract award, before recruiting long-term advisors and otherwise launching the project. An additional fact-finding mission at the start of the contract is not what is needed. If the donor has established good local contacts—officials or consultants—during the definition stage, those contacts can quickly inform the donor of significant changes affecting the project, to allow immediate modification of the statement of work.

DEFINING THE PROJECT'S STRUCTURE

Important questions to be addressed in structuring a project are its relation to other projects in the sector and the expected working relationship with host country consultants.

Finding the Project's Niche

Other donors working in the sector is both a blessing (more resources being brought to bear) and a complication, because of the coordination required. Without effective coordination, multiple projects result in wasteful duplication of effort, with separately funded contractors doing similar work substantially in isolation from each other. They will also have many of the same official clients, thereby taking up an inordinately large amount of the time of key officials in the area.

The following list ranks different organizational arrangements for overall work in a sector from the least to the most complex:

Single donor, single contractor.
Single donor, multiple contractors.

Principal donor among multiple donors, with multiple contractors.
  This arrangement is fairly common in World Bank projects where
  bilateral donors provide help with technical cooperation either in-
  cash or in-kind in both the project appraisal and implementation
  phases.
Multiple donors, multiple contractors.

A clear problem with the multiple donors-multiple contractors model
is ensuring that the program as a whole, however it is divided among
the participating donors, contains all five elements listed as essential
in chapter 1: development of legislation and implementing regulations, demonstration projects, monitoring and evaluation, dissemination, and institutionalization.

  While coordination is the order of the day throughout the donor
community, in practice effective coordination seems to be exceptional. Most resident advisors have had the experience of a project-
definition mission visiting his office, having heard about his program
for the first time from host country officials. Sometimes the new team
is designing a project extremely similar to the one already being implemented. Teams often have not been briefed by their client about the
existing projects before arriving in country and therefore have no
instructions to meet with those implementing the projects. Resident
advisors happily meet with these teams in an attempt to control overt
duplication. They are less happy when they have a similar meeting
with the chief-of-party of a new project with terms of reference very
similar to their own. Finally, lack of coordination in dissemination is
endemic, with each of the donors trying to get maximum exposure
for themselves.

  *Lesson: Donors should work hard at discovering what their counter-
parts are already doing in a sector before launching a new activity. I
acknowledge the difficulty of doing this well for all the possible bilateral programs. Hence, project definition teams sent to the field must
be given the work of identifying other projects as an explicit task in
their terms of reference. A strong effort must be made thereafter to
ensure coordination on an ongoing basis.*[13]

Working with Local Professionals

A key element in structuring a project is to state clearly in the terms
of reference the donor's expectations about the working relations between the contractor and host country professionals. Lethem and
Cooper's (1983: 8) discussion of working relations between foreign

advisors and their clients suggests three models for relations between expatriate consultants and local professional staff or consultants:

1. *No real relations.* The project is essentially implemented by expatriate advisors with some support from professionals who have a clearly subsidiary role that is not designed to evolve into greater responsibilities over the course of the project.
2. *The counterpart-advisor model.* A national staff works in an apprentice capacity to the external specialist.
3. *The collaborative model.* Both national and expatriate staff perform substantive tasks, share responsibility for results, work together as a team, and learn from each other.

In the early years in working in transitional countries, nearly all terms of reference were essentially silent on the role to be played by local staff. Sometimes there was no mention of local professionals at all, aside from official counterparts. There was no prohibition against employing them on the project, but no affirmative provisions either. In some contracts, a level of effort (person month) ceiling on local as well as expatriate consultants was stated, but nothing on expectations about working relations. While it was common for the same contracts to contain tasks for training local officials, bankers, proprietors of small businesses, farmers, and other clearly defined groups, mentoring for local staff was absent. It seems very probable that this was simply a carryover from the contracting practices in less developed countries rather than the result of any conscious decision.

My sense is that beginning in 1995 some of the donors have been clearer about their expectations with respect to the role of local staff and consultants and the contractor's responsibility for producing the desired outcome. In some cases certain types of development of local staff and consultants, including training institutes, are even listed as an explicit project output that will be monitored accordingly. USAID's direction of the Housing Sector Reform Project illustrates the trend.

CASE: In the project's initial contract, signed in September 1992, there was essentially no mention of local staff. In the follow-on contract, signed in September 1995, level of effort figures are stated for local professionals, working either as staff or consultants to the Urban Institute or as subcontractors to the Institute. The substitution of local professionals for expatriates is encouraged. And program institutionalization, including developing local policy and other expertise, is a clearly articulated program objective.

Lesson: Donors must be clear about their expectations regarding the contractor's relations with local professionals in the project. Where mentoring and staff development are an objective and where local professionals are expected to have real responsibility, it must be clearly stated in the contract. This step is critical to capacity building and institutionalization.

THE CONTINUITY PROBLEM

In the interest of fostering competition, donors generally have the rule that consultants or firms who work on the design of a sector technical cooperation project cannot propose on or be included in a proposal for conducting the actual project. These donors believe that those who have participated in the project design would have an unfair advantage in a competition. The rule is strong and it appears to be scrupulously observed by those who have it. Even so, the prohibition is less airtight and less reasonable than might at first appear. For example, if a firm works on design of a technical cooperation project that will be part of a World Bank loan package under a USAID contract, it is not barred from bidding on the World Bank–funded implementation contract. If the same firm worked under contract to the World Bank during preparation, however, it would not be eligible to compete.[14]

The cost of the policy, where it is binding, is the loss to the project of expertise developed during the design stage, including the personal relations established with host country officials. Clearly, this is one reason host country officials complain about the rapid turnover and discontinuity among consultants implementing projects. The rule also restricts who will work on project design. This is a serious matter because project definition can determine the ultimate success of a project; in the entire project it is probably the task requiring the most creativity. This is not the job for the second team.[15]

Some change in the blanket prohibition seems in order, although there is probably no way to fully reconcile the goal of equal competition with capturing the experience of professionals who have participated in a project's design. One option is to limit the amount of work a consulting firm could obtain. Perhaps a contractor who worked on the design phase could be limited in the size of the related implementation contract on which he could bid. Alternatively, there could be a limit on the share of the implementation contract such a firm could receive within a consortium of contractors bidding to do the work—25–35 percent might be a reasonable limit.

If altering the blanket prohibition is not possible, then the best the donor can do is to strengthen the reporting and consultation requirements for project design missions. The background information gathered should be fully reported. There is a tendency now for individual consultants not to be very forthcoming in reporting before the follow-on competitions because they want to maintain some advantage for proposal writing. Hence, the donor's manager may have to be demanding to get a full picture. Moreover, the reporting on host country officials, agencies, and consultants should go beyond the simple listing of "people met" or "consulted" to some commentary on each. This will save the executing contractor an enormous amount of time in starting field operations. Finally, agreements for the design work should include a provision for the team leader, and perhaps others, to spend a day or more with the implementation contractor before the field phase of implementation begins.

Lesson: Donors should rethink their prohibitions against those working on project design being barred from project implementation. At a minimum more of the knowledge gained by consultants doing the design work must be transferred to the implementation team.

Defining sector reform technical cooperation is a tricky business. One must identify a project of genuine interest to the host country client, judge the project's technical and political feasibility, and be convinced that it will have a significant impact on moving the sector away from the command model to one in which prices matter more in allocating resources and production efficiency is enhanced. The process requires that the donor's representatives have a combination of technical competence, seasoned political judgment, and experience operating outside their home country.

Several actions can be taken during project development to increase the project's probability of success:

- Get the responsible and influential host government officials committed to the project.
- Employ and rely upon foreign professionals for technical and policy advice during the design phase and the implementation process; include in the terms of reference prepared for the contractor specific language on how host country professionals are to be used in the project.
- Use the "menu approach" in discussing with the recipients the range of projects with which the donor could offer assistance.

- Be sure the project design is not overtaken by events during the procurement process, by confirming the situation in the sector after conclusion of the competition but before advisors are selected and dispatched to the field.
- Ensure, to the very maximum extent possible, continuity between project design and implementation.

Notes

1. Lethem and Cooper (1983: 17) call this the "state of the art" problem.

2. The need for obtaining a good working relationship as a requirement for successful project design is a common theme in the literature. See, for example, Paul (1990). Buyck (1991) criticizes World Bank institutional development technical cooperation projects for insufficient attention to obtaining firm government commitment to such projects.

3. The Russian health sector reform project cited earlier in the text also used this type of menu approach when negotiating a work program with the four Siberian *oblasts* in which it initially operated demonstration programs.

4. The priorities in the TACIS program are public administration reform; restructuring state enterprises and private sector development; transport and telecommunications infrastructures; energy; nuclear safety and environment; building an effective food production, processing and distribution system; and developing social services and education.

5. In recent years the program has been shifting to a three-year funding cycle.

6. For more on this process, see Hoffman et al. (1996).

7. In its report on the aid programs of seven donors, not including the United States, the GAO (1995b: 50) noted that the "obligate and spend" approach to accountability pushes aid managers to move quickly and militates against "well-designed, -planned, or -implemented" projects.

8. This information is from the Statement of Work for the project, "Development of a Modern Land Use Regulation System in the Russian Federation."

9. Memorandum from John Competellor, RIG/A/Bonn, to Barbara Turner, DAA/PA, of March 10, 1995, "Audit of Selected Privatization and Restructuring Activities in Russia (Project No. 110-0005), Audit Report No. 8-118-95-007."

10. This project is titled, "The Social Assets Conversion (SAC) Project," and the executing agency for the contract is the Russian Privatization Center.

11. A large team of foreign consultants can engender another problem. There is a natural tendency for team members to work with their fellow countrymen. This is certainly understandable, but at the same time it reduces the pressure on the team to seek out local professionals to join the team.

12. We emphasize that flexibility is not a synonym for imprecision. There are many examples of loosely defined projects having difficult teething problems. According to the contractor's staff, USAID Russia's Health Care Financing and Service Delivery Reform project got off to a poor start in part because the Request for Proposals was

vaguely written and permitted a good deal of flexibility in defining specific objectives. This proved to be a problem because the contractor and the USAID program officer set about defining the program differently. The work plan was ultimately used as the vehicle to resolve the divergence of views, but this took more than a year after signing the contract.

13. This point is discussed further in chapter 8.

14. On the other hand, a firm that has been executing a technical cooperation project is not precluded from bidding on a follow-on contract.

15. Lethem and Cooper (1983: 11) also argue that continuity of staff from design to implementation is important for successful technical cooperation projects.

Chapter Four

ACHIEVING CREDIBILITY

Getting technical cooperation projects off to a quick and productive start has been difficult in the former Soviet bloc, a fact reflected in various project evaluations. Because of a sense of lost opportunity in an environment of fast-paced reforms, frustration is common on all sides.

Recipients are frustrated by what they see as promises not fulfilled. In many cases, months pass after ministry officials reach agreement with a project identification mission, and perhaps even sign a formal agreement, before they hear anything. The officials begin thinking of the team as just another group of "donor tourists" who pass through their offices asking questions, dispensing advice gratuitously, and promising help, never to be seen again. Implementation teams can be equally frustrated. They arrive to discover that there is a fundamental misunderstanding with the client ministry about the nature of the project. Frequently conditions in the sector have changed—key legislation has been passed, or economic changes have altered the nature of the problem. The scope of the project must be renegotiated and real work is further delayed. An even worse situation occurs when those designing the project did not correctly identify the host country counterparts. In such a case, the process of project definition must begin afresh after seeking out the "right" people. When one meets the chief-of-party of such projects in the host country one is reminded of the title of a John McPhee book, Looking for a Ship, altered in this case to Looking for a Project. He consults his donor program officer and seeks advice from directors of ongoing projects as he attempts to restructure his project—a process typically taking months.

Start-up problems of these types are wasteful and destructive to the sector reform process. In technical cooperation, as in most other endeavors, a poor start is hard to overcome. Once a project is viewed as largely irrelevant by the host country client, the implementers have ever increasing difficulty obtaining the kind of cooperation needed for genuine success. This chapter provides some lessons in getting a project off to a credible start.

FAST START

Everyone wants to "hit the ground running," but this turns out to require several carefully executed steps, beginning with the nature of the agreement reached between the donor and host country client in defining the project and how quickly the implementation team begins its work.

BE SPECIFIC

Going quickly and effectively to work is facilitated if the initial tasks are well-defined and agreed upon with the host country client in advance. For example, if a demonstration project has been agreed upon, work on structuring the demonstration can start almost immediately, including site selection, meeting with local administrators who will be participating in the pilot, and defining the operational rules.

CASE: As a result of the "menu driven process" described in the last chapter, the Memoranda of Understanding that USAID signed with each of the three participating local governments in the HSRP for Russia listed two or three concrete tasks to be undertaken as part of the technical cooperation program. These projects had already been discussed and agreed upon with those in the local government most responsible for the substantive area involved. Hence, genuine cooperation was expected and, indeed, received when implementation began.

As an example, the agreement with the Moscow government specified as the highest priority a demonstration to introduce private firms, selected through competitions, to maintain units in the municipal housing inventory. The agreement, while signed for the city by Premier Yuri Luzhkov, was confirmed by Alexander Matrosov, the head of the department responsible for housing maintenance. When the team began work on the demonstration some weeks later, full cooperation was received from the department.[1]

Information on project start-up is hard to assemble because there is little interest in this specific phase by evaluators. It is wise to define two or at most three tasks for initial execution within the overall scope of the project. The risk of the need for task redefinition increases exponentially as the number of tasks that are fully specified at the outset is enlarged.

> CASE: The Local Government Initiative (LGI) in Bulgaria found that trying to provide sustained expert advice and assistance on five projects in each of ten municipalities proved to be beyond the resources of the project. And even those services that could be provided tended to overwhelm the reponsible local officials. The result was frustration on the part of the mayors, who perceived that they and their staffs were devoting a great deal of time to working with American and Bulgarian advisors with very few visible results.
>
> With the credibility of the whole LGI at risk, the project's managers renegotiated the work plans with the mayors, usually selecting a single project on which all efforts would be focused. It was also specified that other projects to be initiated (or in some cases continued) after the first project was well underway would have to be in the same program area as the first project so as to maintain focus and momentum. The revised list of priority areas is given in table 4.1, where the program area is given in column 2 and the specific project in column 3.

Precise definition of a task—such as a particular type of demonstration—requires that the project definition team include people with sufficient technical expertise to be able to describe the purposes and the mechanics of such a demonstration in enough detail to "sell" it to the host country counterparts. If such expertise is lacking, then it is probably unwise even to try to formulate specific actions for an early start, or to expect an early start.

Lesson: Project start-up is facilitated by defining a few initial tasks with some precision and for these tasks to be clearly agreed upon by all relevant parties prior to the arrival of the implementation team. Importantly, if the initial tasks are clearly defined, this information can be used in recruiting advisors. Having the right people present to work on the initial tasks obviously accelerates the work.

Define the Doable

The tasks selected for initial work should be those for which the consultant team is likely to be able to make a visible difference within a few months. These will often be demonstration projects, where visibility is certain. Assisting in the definition of reform policy and

Table 4.1 REVISED MUNICIPAL PRIORITIES IN THE USAID-SUPPORTED
BULGARIA LOCAL GOVERNMENT INITIATIVE

Municipality	Priority LGI Program	Phase I Focus LGI Project	Phase II Focus Future LGI Project
Blagoevgrad	upgrading municipal services	improving issuance of plot maps	solid waste; transport planning
Razgrad	upgrading municipal services	modernizing financial management	upgrading civil registration
Rousse	upgrading municipal services	modernizing financial management	[to be determined]
Vidin	upgrading municipal services	modernizing financial management	improving issuance of plot maps
Zlatograd	upgrading municipal services	improving waste disposal and collection	local economic development
Gabrovo	increasing citizen participation	improving service to citizens	improving public access
Haskovo	increasing citizen participation	improving public access	[to be determined]
Stara Zagora	local economic development	preparing downtown revitalization strategy	[to be determined]
Varna	local economic development	creating municipal econ. development office	[to be determined]

Source: Hoffman et al. (1996), Table 2.

drafting the necessary legislation and regulations can clearly also be
a fruitful area.

*Lesson: Define the initial tasks to demonstrate real progress early
in the project. Other activity can and should be going on at the same
time, but concentrate on achieving a demonstrable, even if limited,
success.*

GET TO WORK!

Perhaps the most challenging problem for the donor community is
how to get the implementation team into the field quickly. I addressed
contract delays in chapter 3. These are largely beyond the control of

the implementers. But the results of delay can certainly be aggravated by further delay after contract signing. The troops may come prepared to fight the wrong battle. Worse, the clients may stop counting on the assistance. It may be that they even ask another donor for the same project assistance, assuming that nothing will come of the earlier promises.

CASE: The GAO (1995) evaluation of USAID projects in the Russian Federation is peppered with delays of six months in the arrival of the resident advisors *after* the contract for assistance services has been signed. Other examples for Russia include the case of Research Triangle Institute, which signed a contract for a technical cooperation project in the municipal finance area in October 1993 and whose advisors arrived in January—a four-month delay. The same dates apply to Burns & Roe fielding resident advisors for a USAID energy sector project.

The probability of project success is certainly increased by rapid follow-up of the project identification mission with implementation. How to do it is the question.

CASE: The HSRP in Russia succeeded in keeping the period between project identification and initial implementation brief. Project identification, including the signing of agreements, was accomplished in March–April 1992. After a few weeks' absence, the team leader returned to Moscow in May with other consultants to begin work on specific tasks set out in the agreements. During the design mission, local Russian professionals were identified and recruited to assemble background materials and to work with the team during the May mission. Two tasks undertaken early were starting work with the Moscow City Government on the housing maintenance demonstration and with Federation agencies on the major housing reform law, which would be written over the next several months. With the exception of a few weeks during June and July, the team leader remained in Russia through the signing of the implementation contract in early September to push these projects forward. There was essentially no break between the design and implementation phases of the project.

How was this possible? It goes back again, at least in part, to how the contract was drawn. At the time the Urban Institute worked for USAID in the urban sector under a contract which covered the entire world. Task orders, which could be processed quickly, were written to the Institute for the work in Russia. While the initial work in Russia went forward, USAID prepared the Request for Proposals and held a competition for the full, three-year implementation contract. Under the then-applicable contracting rules, the Urban Institute was permitted to compete. Under today's USAID rules, which are similar to those of other donors, the Institute could not compete.[2]

Maintaining the momentum achieved during the project identification mission until full implementation begins is crucial. The most obvious option is for some members of the design team to participate in follow-on work during the contracting process, assuming they have the right skills. USAID has now developed another contracting vehicle, the "omnibus contract," which is designed to overcome the lag problem posed by the need for competitively bid procurements. Under this arrangement contractors, usually consortia of contractors, compete on the basis of general qualifications and price for the right to respond to requests from USAID for specific services. USAID qualifies a substantial number of contractors in the first phase and then holds rapid, more limited competitions for the specific work. The task orders issued are supposed to be for fairly short-term projects—typically in the range of six months—but this appears to be a "soft budget constraint."[3]

CASE: In one case the projects were defined by a group composed of people from USAID, the State Property Committee of the Russian Federation, and the Harvard Institute for International Development (HIID), which participates under a cooperative agreement with USAID.[4] New projects were defined on a regular semi-annual basis. HIID did most of the actual drafting of the Statements of Work. These were then used by USAID in the competitions among selected firms covered by the omnibus contract.[5]

Other donors typically do not have such flexible contracting vehicles, meaning that full competitions, which take at least several months, are still the rule.

Consultants can also take steps themselves to prepare for making rapid progress as soon as they arrive in country. Three opportunities, all used in HSRP, come quickly to mind. First, read and master whatever germane background materials can be found. As remarkable as it may seem, most consultants arrive in the field badly prepared. If there is not much on a specific topic for the country of assignment (for example, Armenia) one can learn a lot about the old system by reading a treatise for the Soviet Union and learning what sectoral reforms other former Soviet bloc countries have undertaken. Second, ask local (host country) professionals to prepare background materials and even begin some preliminary tasks. A good team will have identified competent local professionals during the design mission and could get them to work as soon as a contract is signed or even earlier if some "bridge funding" is provided by the donor. Third, look for materials about relevant reforms in other countries and have them translated. Being able to distribute papers in the local language at initial meetings impresses to the client that the consultant thought enough about what he was to do to come ready to work.

BEING RESPONSIVE

In addition to rapid project start-up and a demonstration of genuine progress in the first few months, for the technical cooperation team to be responsive to its counterparts' legitimate requests for help is also vital to achieving credibility with host country officials. By legitimate I mean requests that are consistent with the scope and spirit of the tasks defined in the agreement between the donor and host country and in the implementation team's terms of reference. Being responsive is key to establishing a close working relationship with the counterparts (i.e., to being a "member of the team" rather than an individual or firm doing something useful but in relative isolation from the main business of the ministry, agency, bank, or enterprise).

Typically the requests for help are modest but often urgent. They usually, but by no means always, result from imperatives in the policy development process.

CASE: In October 1992 the Minister of Construction on a Friday afternoon asked the HSRP team to prepare for him procedures on how to hold a competition for the award of contracts for government-sponsored construction. The possible shift to competitive awards was a major change from the old Soviet system and was viewed as potentially important. Because the minister said he had to have the response by Tuesday, the team worked over the weekend to produce a quite complete description of procedures. The document was translated on Monday and delivered on time to a grateful, and surprised, minister.

CASE: In November 1992 the First Deputy Minister of Finance asked the HSRP for a statement on a housing finance strategy for the Russian Federation, to be prepared within two days. There was little in the Soviet system that would pass for a housing finance system in the Western sense, as most residential construction was simply funded directly or indirectly by the state. The HSRP included a housing finance component, however, and work had begun on this topic a couple of months earlier; so the team had been thinking about the issue. The Deputy Minister had a genuine interest in housing reform and saw an opportunity for advancing the reform agenda if he had a blueprint on how to proceed. The document was prepared and delivered on time.

CASE: In October 1993, following the disbanding of the Supreme Soviet by President Yeltsin and the storming of the White House by the army, the Acting Prime Minister saw the opportunity for enactment of several Presidential Decrees that would advance housing reform before the new parliament would convene the following January. He requested the Ministries of Construction and Finance and the Economic Reform Working Center to nominate possible decrees and then to prepare the text of the decrees that his office approved. Because of good working relations with all three entities, the Urban Institute team was invited to be a full partner in the work. The first task was to draft within two days its own list of decree topics. This was done on time, as were other drafting tasks assigned to it. And the team retained its credibility in the eyes of its Russian partners. At the end, two Presidential Decrees were issued. One enables the creation of condominium associations (primarily from buildings containing privatized units); the other creates a subsidy program that provides downpayment assistance to home purchasers who are on the waiting list for municipal housing, i.e., the program permits families to combine their own funds with the downpayment subsidy in order to obtain housing to jump the queue rather than waiting to be assigned a municipal unit, for which the local government pays the full cost.[6]

CASE: In 1995 the mortgage subsidiary of the East Siberian Commercial Bank was negotiating a possible loan for mortgage lending from The U.S.-Russia Investment Fund (TUSRIF). The Urban Institute had been involved earlier, helping TUSRIF identify candidate banks and providing information on housing lending in Russia. The mortgage subsidiary asked the Urban Institute to review some of the financial materials it had prepared for the negotiations on an urgent basis. This was done and the relations between the bank and team further strengthened.

Lesson: To enhance its credibility the technical cooperation team should seek opportunities to assist its clients with critical tasks. Often this will require the team extending itself—working over the weekend or having to push hard to meet urgent client requests and continue progress on its demonstration program. An important result of helping in a pinch is that word spreads that the team is serious about its work. This has the snowballing effect of helping other aspects of the technical cooperation program go more easily.

THE RECEPTIVE CLIENT

An interested client is the *sine qua non* of successful consulting— whether in Russia, India, or Great Britain. Real interest requires something beyond the minimum requirement for project feasibility established during the design stage. As argued in chapter 2, those implementing sector technical cooperation programs in the former Soviet bloc have the advantage of much more often having truly interested clients than those operating in other parts of the world.

CASE: When International Finance Corporation instituted an agricultural land sales program in Russia's Nizhni Novgorod *Oblast*, it enjoyed the strong support of the *Oblast's* Governor. His support was critical in pushing the program forward with the region's local administrators.

CASE: The HSRP had the good fortune of beginning operations when Russian sectoral leaders, both in the City of Moscow and the Russian Federation, were ready for change and receptive to advice. Although a World Bank staff member had spent a half-dozen months in Russia scattered over several missions as an advisor for the housing sector, he was shifted to tasks in other countries. Hence, the HSRP has enjoyed the luxury of being *the* advisor to an active and committed client.

An interested client, however, must still be convinced that proposed reforms can work in his country, region, or municipality. When the consultant offers new ideas, he should describe them fully in the host country context and, if at all possible, demonstrate that other countries of the former Soviet bloc have adopted or are considering similar reforms.

> CASE: In the HSRP it was clear early on that raising rents on state housing was a key factor in rationalizing the use of the housing stock. It was also clear, in turn, that a housing allowance would have to be implemented at the time rents were raised in order to protect the poor from spending an excessive share of their incomes on housing. There was skepticism from the Russian side about the effectiveness of the package of rent increases and housing allowances in both raising revenues and sheltering the poor. Analysis for Hungary led the team to believe that the total revenue from increasing rents in that country would comfortably exceed the cost of the housing allowance payments, so that cities would have funds left over to improve maintenance or reduce the public cost of the subsidies to housing. But the Russian clients understood that there were good reasons why this might not hold in Russia, one being the much larger share of all housing owned by the state in Russia (67 percent in Russia versus 20 percent in Hungary in 1990). So, instead of relying on the findings for Hungary, new simulations were done, first for the City of Moscow and later for the municipalities of Novosibirsk and Ufa. They did, indeed, reveal marked differences from the Hungarian case. They were also valuable in persuading Federation officials that a housing allowance program would work in Russia, even if at greater public cost than in Hungary.[7] This evidence proved decisive in the debate about whether the Government would include the provision for raising rents in the seminal housing reform law.

Lesson: Tailor advice and recommendations for the local context, even if it requires a good deal of extra work. Going out of one's way to make the advice immediately applicable helps win rapport with the client by convincing him that the consulting team understands the local situation and that the team genuinely wants to provide usable assistance.

COMPETENCE ON THE GROUND

Experienced senior managers of international technical cooperation programs appreciate the key role of the chief-of-party. As one person put it, the leader's "personality, charisma, drive, intellectual ability, international experience, creativity, political acuity, and other individual characteristics can make or break a successful technical assistance foray." At the same time, the examples in the previous section make manifest the need for the team to have genuine competence on the ground, i.e., people who can respond with alacrity to requests for substantive assistance. When the urgent request comes from the minister, for example, it is unacceptable for an absent chief-of-party to respond that a short-term expert can be on-site in the next three or four weeks.

For small projects (i.e., projects with one or two resident advisors), this requires a difficult set of staffing decisions. On the one hand, the project needs broad-based leadership with a good deal of experience in the sector and in dealing with contractors, donors, government officials, and other clients. Seasoned judgment is extremely important when working in new surroundings and managing a complex project. Similarly, the ability to see "the whole field," to have a vision of the whole project and to understand when program adjustments are necessary, is often critical to project success. Typically, the more of the latter type of experience a person possesses, the less sharp his narrow technical skills. But on the other hand, project leadership also requires strong technical competence—people who can do the detailed design work, explain the intricacies of the proposed demonstration, or draft the key sections of implementing regulations and prepare the associated guidelines for those administering the program.[8]

Candidates having all the skills are often not available, and a decision on which type of strength to emphasize becomes inescapable. Discussions with donor managers with vast experience in implementing technical cooperation projects—such as USAID's Mission Director in Russia, Jim Norris—indicate that if a choice is unavoidable, choosing greater experience and judgment over technical skills is generally right. The potential problem with technical specialists is that they can focus too exclusively on technical issues—while the project may be losing its sponsorship or becoming irrelevant without the chief-of-party really being aware of it. The danger of frictions with host country officials is also progressively reduced as the overseas experience of an expert increases.

This points to a third critical attribute of the team leader: experience in working outside his home country. There is nothing magic about operating in a new country, but it also is not merely a question of intuition. The chief-of-party must know how to deal with his host country counterparts and with his donor clients—two groups that frequently do not have the same objectives in mind. Knowing how to get things done efficiently is also a must—for example, hiring competent local professionals, renting office space, organizing furniture and office supplies, getting long-term visas, opening bank accounts, and a million other details. It is all to easy too get bogged down in the logistics, with a corresponding reduction in project productivity.

CASE: In 1994 in Russia, U.S. contractors and grantees organized the Association of American Providers of International Assistance to Russia to address common problems experienced in operating in the country. One of the group's tasks was to communicate with USAID about those problems they believed the agency could help them resolve. Reflecting in part the lack of experience outside the United States, the list included registering their firm in Russia as a "representative office," finding office space, getting goods through customs, and the like. Those firms with greater experience in other countries undertook to resolve these problems by themselves. Those requesting help from USAID were typically new to the international arena.

The conundrum of broad experience (including overseas work) versus direct technical competence for the task at hand was particularly acute in the early years of implementing technical cooperation projects in the former Soviet bloc. First, almost no one had relevant experience in these countries. Second, the cadre of professionals with experience working in developing countries frequently had not worked on the problems for which help was needed in the former Soviet bloc. In the housing sector, for example, work in developing nations often focused on organizing the construction of very basic housing for low-income families in urban areas ("sites and services" projects), upgrading squatter settlements, developing realistic land use systems, and creating a housing finance system, often in the face of high inflation and excessive government intervention in financial markets. Of these areas, only the last is relevant for most of the former Soviet bloc.[9]

In order to field experts with relevant technical knowledge the donors generally contracted with firms with little if any overseas experience. Often they were not truly expert in the task at hand (e.g., privatization), but possessed the general financial and managerial skills thought needed to get the job done. Learning-by-doing, thus, became essential, which was both expensive to the donors and frustrating to recipients.

Although one would expect the dearth of experts with genuine experience in Eastern Europe and the Newly Independent States to be a thing of the past, in reality it remains something of a problem. Many experts who worked in the region for a couple of years—caught up in the excitement of the moment and enjoying the break in their routine—do not want to make such consulting a career. For this reason, staffing technical assistance projects remains a challenge.

How, then, can a small technical cooperation team with an experienced, broad-gauge chief-of-party but little technical expertise respond to the type of urgent requests I have been discussing? The most obvious response is for the project to build up a record of having worked with local professionals, so that the local people can handle such requests subject to review by the team leader. For requests beyond the experience of the local experts, the only good fallback is for the project team's home office to have technical back-up with which to respond. This back-up person needs significant in-country experience and thorough familiarity not only with the sector prior to reforms but also with developments since reforms began. Through e-mail connections, a fast turnaround on a written product is possible. The face-to-face discussion of details will be missing, but that will be inevitable given staffing constraints on site, and is considerably less dangerous than an insufficiently experienced chief-of-party at the scene.

> CASE: In the HSRP, the chief-of-party had substantial overseas experience and was able to handle directly the urgent requests for policy advice in the first year or so. Thereafter, Russian colleagues were capable of drafting and presenting policy reform positions. On many legislative questions input was obtained from the project's legal advisor, who was stationed in the United States but visited Russia several times a year.

Notes

1. This process worked well in two of the three Russian cities where agreements had been signed for the HSRP. However, in Ekaterinburg the projects defined in the pilot were not pursued. The history is unclear. The advisor initially sent by USAID to the city for a two-month trial period did not continue in the post. After a several-month interval a new resident advisor arrived to take up his duties. It is unclear why the new

advisor did not pursue the agenda in the initial agreement; over six months had passed since the agreement had been signed.

2. In Eastern Europe the pattern of a USAID contractor doing design and initial implementation work under an already existing flexible contract and then bidding on a contract for further implementation was not exceptional. This was permitted largely because of the urgency of getting the work underway. The "flexible contract" was a so-called "Indefinite Quantity Contract" or IQC, under which one or more firms wins a competition to provide services in a particular area, for example, health or housing or small business development in a particular region or anywhere in the world. The guaranteed amount of work was typically small. The Agency could then write task orders under the contract directing the firm to do work in a particular country. The task orders were limited to three or four months in duration.

3. In Russia USAID has actually had two generations of these contracts, which are structured somewhat differently in terms of the way in which USAID commits funds to contractors under the task orders. The more recent version gives USAID more control over the use of the money and is generally a better vehicle.

4. A cooperative agreement contains provisions that place it between a contract and a grant, in terms of the freedom given to the firm.

5. This description is contained in Competellor (1995), Annex III, p. 6.

6. Further discussion of housing reform in the Russian Federation is given in Annex A. Also see Kosareva, Puzanov, and Suchkov (1996).

7. Details of this work are reported in Struyk, Kosareva et al. (1993).

8. There is substantial literature on the qualities which long-term advisors should possess. See, for example, Lethem and Cooper (1983).

9. A limited exception to the "no relevant experience" dictum is the work on industrial privatization whether in developing nations (e.g., Argentina) or industrialized countries (e.g., Great Britain).

Part Three

ONGOING OPERATIONS

Chapter Five

DELIVERING THE SERVICES

This chapter shifts from the rigors of project launch to factors important for successful delivery of services in a sector reform program during "steady state" operations. Topics range from the type of foreign team presence appropriate to coordination of multi-project sector reform programs.[1]

IN-COUNTRY PRESENCE

At the beginning of the transition of Eastern European countries from the Soviet economic and political system to more Western-oriented principles, as I note earlier, the common view among donors was that the transition would be swift. It followed that the expense of setting up permanent donor missions in these countries should be avoided and, similarly, that resident advisors would be unnecessary. Advice could be provided by experts visiting the countries on short-term missions and in five years, the whole task would be over.

Reality has turned out very differently. The assumptions underlying the structure of the early sector reform projects have been roundly criticized for being ineffective and the donor agencies have responded by changing their mode of operation.[2]

A full sector reform project that includes the five elements enunciated earlier—policy and legislation development, demonstration projects, monitoring and evaluation, dissemination, and institutionalization—is a large and complex undertaking. Managing such a project on an in-out basis is rarely feasible. The demands for actively participating in policy development, working on the design of demonstration projects with host country officials, trouble-shooting problems during implementation, and being available to present project findings at in-country conferences and seminars cannot be done on a part-time basis. This truth is not changed by the presence in the country of donor agency staff: they cannot and should not try to substitute for the more technically proficient senior management of contracted firms.

In addition, sector technical assistance projects often need "mid-course corrections." A part-time chief-of-party will have greater difficulty than his resident counterpart in anticipating the need for change before it becomes acute. Delayed adjustments can be expensive, both in conflict with host country clients and in pouring resources into unproductive activities.

CASE: USAID's health sector reform project in Russia had to be adjusted when it became clear that the Ministry of Health would not cooperate fully with the project, leading *oblast* and municipal governments to be reluctant to undertake broad reform demonstration projects.

CASE: In the part of the HSRP dedicated to addressing reform of housing finance, the team had advocated that banks use a particular type of mortgage instrument (the dual-rate mortgage, a loan denominated in local currency that defers some of the payments due from the borrower in the early years of the loan term to later years when the borrower's income is higher), which worked well in an economic climate characterized by high and volatile inflation. Software to service this type of loan was developed by the project and offered to banks. The banks, however, were more comfortable using dollar-denominated loans, which were simple compared to the other instrument. The project team adjusted by adding the capability of servicing the dollar-denominated loan to the loan servicing software. This showed responsiveness to the banks' needs and a willingness to remain relevant to them. It also, by having both types of instruments in a common software package, made the cost of eventually switching to the dual-rate mortgage modest.

The only exceptions to the rule that an in-country presence is required are when (1) the donor has not defined an overall sector reform program but decides to execute a discrete project in a sector that may contribute to overall reform or (2) the donor divides sectoral reform into several limited and discrete projects. In both cases, use of short-term consultants rather than residents can be cost-effective because the projects are so restricted.

CASE: The British Know How Fund has a finance project in the Russian Federation under which an England-based consultant spends two or three weeks a month in Russia giving expert advice. Most of this time is spent working with the St. Petersburg government on its program of raising funds through issuing bonds. The balance is spent working on mortgage lending operations with the Nizhni Novgorod Interregional Land Bank. It is possible that each project may lead to the demonstration of innovations that will be picked up by the rest of the country. Obviously, they do not constitute a sector reform program.

The importance of in-country residency should not be interpreted as implying that the technical cooperation team should single-handedly carry out various tasks. The more responsibility that can be assigned to local counterparts in government or other institutions, the greater will be their commitment to the endeavor. Indeed, if they do not assume responsibility quickly, the project should put this part of the implementation plan on hold.

CASE: In the HSRP, counterparts were given as much responsibility as possible. In working with commercial banks to introduce mortgage lending, the HSRP team would visit the bank periodically and provide training and information. These sessions were complemented with formal training courses. Still, it was up to the bank to get its program organized and off the ground. If a bank was slow to take the next step, then the team would stop visiting the bank until it was again ready to proceed. Occasional phone contact was maintained in the meantime. A similar procedure was used in working with municipal governments to create the first condominium associations. Under the Presidential Decree that permitted formation of condominium associations, local governments had to pass several normative (legislative) acts to make formation possible in each city. The Urban Institute team advised officials about the contents of these acts, provided model documents, and responded to requests for specific help. If the acts were not developed, the team would stay in contact with the officials but stop the on-site visits until progress was made. If a bank or city lost interest completely, the team moved on to others.

For both banks and local governments the approach was the same: place primary responsibility for action with the client. The team's work was to be helpful in many ways but not to replace bankers or local officials in implementing the innovations.

People moving in and out of the country and working on fairly isolated projects find it hard to keep abreast of sector developments and, thus, to contribute what they learn from their work to the broader process of reform, including changing legislation and regulations. For this reason their contribution is more effective when it is part of a larger sector reform operation.

CASE: The Housing Sector Reform Program employed a part-time lawyer, Steve Butler, who was stationed in the United States. He worked closely with the key Russian policy analyst, Nadezhda Kosareva. Butler drafted most of the legislation the program initiated in response to government requests, but it was Kosareva's task to work with Russian government and State Duma clients to shape the draft into a form more technically and politically suitable for Russia. Lessons learned from the demonstration projects were fed into the process at this point. Butler visited Russia several times a year to keep posted and to hold face-to-face discussions with Russian lawyers and officials. The two worked effectively in tandem.

Lesson: Comprehensive sector reform technical cooperation projects require a resident advisor to coordinate all activities in the project and to make needed ongoing adjustments to the work program. But host country clients should be given real responsibility for making changes. Use of expatriate advisors should be limited to those tasks that local staff, consultants, or firms cannot do. Since there will be numerous tasks for which short-term advice is appropriate, however, projects should not adopt a "residents only" policy. It is both expensive and inefficient.

WHY LOCAL PROFESSIONALS ARE SO IMPORTANT

Possibly the single most important action a manager can take to ensure the success of a sector technical cooperation project is to make maximum use of local professionals. Why? Four reasons are paramount. First, it will enhance project efficiency. Since most reforms are partial, it is imperative that those designing the change understand how the change will fit with the old system: at a minimum the new, interim system must be workable. Local professionals know more about how the old system worked than an outsider can hope to master even in several years. Local professionals employed by donor contractors also have very valuable contacts, because most were employed by prestigious research institutes prior to the transition. Some of their colleagues migrated to government positions when the government changed; some are in very senior positions. But beyond these "policy contacts," acquaintance with and knowledge about the administrators in the relevant ministries and municipal agencies is invaluable in making appointments and obtaining information.

Second, a day of local staff time is dramatically cheaper than that of an equivalent expatriate. In the HSRP, a senior Russian staff member cost the project about $185 per day, including all social security taxes, income taxes, and Urban Institute overheads. The cost of a mid-level U.S. staff member resident in the country, including various allowances, was about $550 per day; a senior U.S. advisor would cost twice this.[3] With savings of this magnitude, project resources go much further. Instead of two demonstration sites, for example, a project can handle four; and the more numerous the successful sites, the greater the credibility of the reform to other cities.

Third, local professionals can do some things that are inherently impossible for outsiders, even those with good command of the local language. For instance, government officials are often more comfortable debating policy options or doing detailed drafting among their fellow countrymen. Obviously this is especially true if the foreign advisor is not fluent in the local language. But even if language is not a barrier, local professionals know the history of the prior debates and have an implicit feel for what is politically feasible that the expatriate advisor cannot acquire until after a year or two in the country. Because advisors are there to advise, they will intervene in what they believe are constructive ways. But this may slow down the discussion as points have to be explained to him to the extent that he may be viewed as a greater cost than benefit. Rather than trying to force the advisor into the process, it is better to mentor a staff member to be a constructive participant and for the advisor to rely on one-on-one meetings to get particularly critical points across.

Fourth, employing local professionals is fundamental to institutionalizing reform. A core of professionals knowledgeable and articulate about the reforms must exist outside government as well as within. These professionals will continue to act as trainers, researchers, and participants in the policy process after the expatriates are through. (See chapter 7 for further discussion of institutionalization.)[4]

The alternatives for engaging local professionals in sector reform technical cooperation projects can be divided into three categories:

1. Hiring local professionals onto the consulting firm staff,
2. Hiring individual consultants or local consulting firms to work for the implementing contractor,
3. Engineering a donor-arranged marriage between a local consulting firm and the implementing contractor.

The implementing contractor's choice between the first two options should depend on the amount of professional development (mentoring) believed necessary to accomplish institutionalization, the capabilities of existing consulting/research firms, and the consistency with which services of a particular type are going to be needed—the more episodic the need, the stronger the argument for using consultants or consulting firms.

CASE: In the USAID-sponsored project on regulating natural monopolies in Russia, the contractor, IRIS,[5] concentrates on compiling diagnostic reports on the sector and commenting on draft legislation. Its strategy in part has been to contract with individual researchers within the country and to work with them to produce reports meeting international standards. Through this activity, the project's objective is development of competent independent policy analysts.

CASE: Taking an alternative approach, the HSRP has emphasized staff recruitment to meet the needs of its ambitious program of demonstration projects and direct assistance to many cities and banks, as well as to support development of the new legal base. Having these professionals in-house facilitated staff training and mentoring. At the same time, the project contracts with individuals and institutes for household surveys in support of monitoring and evaluation activities and conducting freestanding studies. The project also hires consultants through firms for extended periods when this is the only available means of obtaining their services.

Arranged, or at least recommended, marriages, which are the least common of the three alternatives, may be a particularly valuable mechanism in countries where technical cooperation programs have been underway for several years. In this scheme, the donor links a foreign firm selected through competition with a local firm, which will be its partner during project execution. A voluntary arrangement is preferable but arranged contact has also worked in practice.

CASE: The Russian Privatization Center (RPC) was formed as a private nonprofit entity by the State Property Committee of the Russian Federation, with the backing of USAID and the active assistance of the Harvard Institute for International Development (HIID), to help implement the country's mass privatization program. RPC's activities included helping USAID define and coordinate projects in the privatization portfolio and work with USAID-supported and other contractors in implementing privatization assistance projects. During implementation, HIID and RPC functioned as part of the State Property Committee staff and had the full confidence of the Russian Federation for defining donor assistance projects and overseeing their execution.

The privatization program originally focused on enterprise privatization. When mass (voucher) privatization concluded in July 1994, the State Property Committee added new tasks to its agenda, including post-privatization assistance to enterprises, development of the capital market (to provide investment finance to private firms), and land privatization and associated development of a private real estate sector.

The Real Estate Information System (REIS) project was part of the real estate program. In this case RPC worked with the firms selected to execute the project, Chemonics and Arthur Anderson, to implement information systems in several cities as the precursor to and basis for a full title registration system. RPC staff screened candidate cities as to their interest in and likely dedication to implementing the system, while USAID, with advice from the U.S. firms, made the final decision. Each REIS project city had a team leader, an American, and a city team co-leader, a Russian. As the Americans were phased out in the city, the co-leader became the leader. The American chief-of-party for Chemonics rated this working arrangement as effective.

A similar result is occurring in other countries. Typically, the partner is a local consulting firm that emerged in the early days of the transition and has gradually enhanced its technical skills and learned the in and outs of contracting with donor agencies. Such firms now work closely with different donors, providing both logistical support and substantive expertise. They include the Metropolitan Research Institute in Budapest, which works with the USAID housing sector and municipal reform projects and with some World Bank missions, as well as taking other discrete donor assignments. Similarly, MTK Konsult in Sofia works with the USAID municipal and real estate reform projects. Again, those who have worked with these firms are impressed with the technical proficiency of the staff and the efficiency with which they operate in their countries.

The joint consulting firm model has a good deal to commend it, if properly used. Local professionals can handle the tasks at which they will be particularly efficient, including screening candidate sites or institutions for demonstration projects and training institutes for offering courses. The tendency of foreign firms to assign the logistical and routine service delivery tasks to the local consultants, and to keep the more developmental tasks exclusively for themselves, should be firmly resisted. While better than an exclusively foreign operation, it is a disappointing outcome because of the forgone opportunity to provide new work opportunities to local professionals.

The existence of local consulting firms in every country with expertise in various areas cannot be taken for granted, however. The huge international consulting firms—such as Price Waterhouse, the Barents Group (KPMG), and Deloitte Touche—are filling this void in the more business-oriented substantive areas. These firms are establishing field offices in the principal cities in the countries of the former Soviet bloc and staffing them with local professionals, usually with the exception of the consulting operations and overall office head. The core expatriate presence is supplemented by substantial short-term help. It is unclear to what extent local staff are subject to a "glass ceiling" through this arrangement. And coverage of various sectors is still far from comprehensive. As discussed in chapter 7, a legitimate goal of a technical reform project is to foster development of new local firms.

Regardless of the structure of the arrangement, the working style of out-of-country advisors will significantly affect the productivity of local professionals. As one of my colleagues said, "the expat has to quickly establish himself as a coworker (one of the boys, if you'll excuse me) and not a super expert from on high."

The logical limit to the involvement of local firms is for the donors to begin contracting directly for services with the more capable firms. The European Union prides itself on being a leader in this regard. The PHARE program reported in 1995 that Polish consulting firms were engaged in more than 3,000 projects across Eastern and Central Europe, and that Hungarian companies had won more EU contracts than all of the Spanish, Danish, Greek, and Irish ones combined.[6] At present, the pattern is for firms from the more advanced parts of the region to work not only in their own countries but also in those less far along in the reform process.

Despite the promising stories just recounted, most contractors still do not work naturally with local professionals. Learning to recruit them may take real effort, although in countries where well-established local firms now operate this should not be a very high hurdle. But it is also the case, and more to the point, that the individual team leaders simply do not make recruitment of local professionals a priority.[7]

Lesson 1: Heavy involvement of local professionals in sector technical cooperation projects will increase project efficiency and productivity and should be an integral part of all but the smallest, most limited projects.

Lesson 2: Few contractors will naturally give a major role in the implementation of sector reform projects to local professionals. Therefore, donor contracts should contain provisions requiring it, and donor oversight of implementation should include this area. A promising idea, already embodied in some contracts, is to require that the share of professional services to be delivered by local professionals increase over the life of the project.

TRACKING DEVELOPMENTS

Covered under this heading are (1) monitoring (keeping track of what is happening) and (2) evaluation (rigorous assessment of the impacts of an intervention or change in policy). Both activities provide project managers (contractors, donors, and host country officials) important information about the pace and impacts of reform. Without such tracking, there are two dangers. The next steps in reform may be unclear or, if clear, may be resisted on the basis of anecdotal evidence about adverse impacts of reforms to date. Or ignorance of the facts may lead managers to believe all is going well, when in fact broad-based resistance to further reforms is developing because of real problems.

In Russia, with the exception of the HSRP, I identified no sector reform technical assistance project that included sector monitoring and evaluation as an explicit part of its work program. My own knowledge and information from advisors working in Eastern Europe lead to a broadly similar conclusion there also. One exception is a USAID-supported project in Hungary. Two household surveys were undertaken to monitor developments in the housing sector in Budapest; and funds were provided to evaluate the demonstration housing allowance and housing management programs in Szolnok. The overall project also mounted a large effort to compute "housing indicators" to measure changes in the sector over time.

Monitoring

This means keeping track of developments in the sector generally and in the areas in which the project is working in particular.[8] Some monitoring activities can use information already available. But others require new information. The most efficient way to describe these further is to give examples from the HSRP, which has carried out a fairly broad range of monitoring activities. Among those addressing general developments in the housing sector and which drew on information from secondary sources are:

(a) a semi-annual annotated listing of Federation-level reform laws in the sector and a more restricted listing of exemplar provincial and municipal reform laws;

(b) periodic updating of a chart showing the number of housing units privatized nationally and in Moscow since January 1992;

(c) a monograph prepared annually reviewing housing reform in Russia since July 1991.

Monitoring activity requiring new data includes gathering data about twice a year from a sample of some 35 cities on the number of condominiums created; preparing a spreadsheet periodically to track competitions to maintain municipal housing in several cities; a survey of banks advertising housing lending to learn about typical terms and conditions for such loans; household surveys in three cities in 1994 and 1995 to determine the extent to which households had heard about the availability of housing allowances and to estimate the rate of participation among income-eligible households; and an annual survey of the occupants of about 2,500 dwelling units in Moscow used to monitor mobility rates, housing expense-to-income ratios, the characteristics of those who privatized their units and reasons for others not privatizing, market selling and renting of privatized units, and housing allowance participation.

A reasonable question is whether all of this activity has done more than make possible preparing up-to-date reports on sector developments. The response is "yes."

CASE: From the assessment of the housing allowance program, analysis of the survey results for the cities of Vladimir and Gorodetz showed that in the fall of 1994 program knowledge and participation rates were low in the first year of the five-year program to raise rents to cover full operating costs (Struyk and Puzanov 1995). This meant that many households eligible for housing allowance payments were not receiving them. Obviously, this could lead to broad resistance to further rent increases and thereby halt this critical element of reform. These results were communicated to the Minister of Construction and to the relevant Deputy Governor in every province with the strong advice that the next round of rent increases, generally scheduled for early 1995, be accompanied by an aggressive information campaign about housing allowance availability. In fact, many localities did conduct the information campaigns and participation rates rose substantially.[9]

CASE: On housing finance, the project was soliciting the support of the Union of Association of Russian Banks for housing legislation that was pending in the State Duma. In explaining the importance of the legislation, being able to cite concrete figures on the extent of long-term housing lending by Russian commercial banks was pivotal in convincing the Association's president that this was a matter of importance to his membership. These were data that the project had compiled because no public agency tracked housing lending.

CASE: The broad pattern in Russia was for the privatization rate of municipal housing to be substantially higher than for the housing under the control of state enterprises. The project learned through surveys that closely monitored housing unit privatizations that many families had been discouraged from pursuing privatization because of misinformation. A couple of years later, when enterprises that had themselves been privatized transferred their housing to municipal governments, an advertising campaign was organized to promote unit privatization among tenants of this housing. From the monitoring data, it was also known that blue collar workers were the most reluctant to privatize. Consequently, all the TV and radio public service announcements were designed to target this group.

Program Evaluation

The focus here is not on donor assessments of project or program performance—a process that typically measures project results against "performance indicators" set forth in the project contract and often focuses on the process of delivering assistance. Rather, the focus is on analyses undertaken by or on behalf of the implementation team to answer the question: What happened as the result of a specific reform? What was the impact? In numerous cases being able to respond to this question is key to being able to go further. Process and impact evaluations in this context are tools in the implementation process.

CASE: The first demonstration project in the HSRP was the introduction of private firms, selected through competitions, to maintain municipal housing in Moscow. The initial contracts with three firms were signed by a city agency in March 1993 to maintain 2,000 units. Another 5,000 units were placed under contract in September of the same year. In both instances a two-wave survey of residents was conducted—prior to the shift to the private firms and about three months after. Residents of the same dwelling units were interviewed in each wave. Respondents were asked straightforward questions about conditions in their buildings, such as, "In the last month how often were the lights in your hallway not working?" The results showed dramatic improvement in the quality of basic maintenance provided by the private firms over the short term—results that were instrumental in persuading the mayor to extend the demonstration to other sites and, in 1995, to issue a decree calling for all the city's two million units to be brought under private, competitive maintenance by the end of 1998. The same results have been important in convincing administrators in other cities to try selection of firms through competition to replace the state firms, which have enjoyed monopolies for decades.

CASE: The health sector reform project in Russia, for which Abt Associates was the contractor, set up a before-and-after monitoring program to measure impacts in the demonstration programs. In the area of improving the quality of care, the measures tracked over time included the rates at which patients in hospitals acquired infections and vaginal delivery complications. In the areas of financing and resource management, indicators included the ratio of outpatient to inpatient expenditures, the ratio of involvement of specialists to generalists, the rate at which patients were referred to specialists, and hospital days per 1,000 population.[10]

Self-evaluation by the contractor's own team, as in the cases just recounted, always raises questions of objectivity. Here the data collection was contracted out but the analysis was done by the Urban Institute team. (In the Abt case, hospitals gathered the data and Abt analyzed it.) While a more arm's length arrangement is desirable, organizing it would have been complex, time consuming, and possibly more expensive. To date the veracity of the findings has not been questioned. There's an inevitable trade-off here. Raising the requirements (and the total effort) of carrying out evaluations will result in fewer being undertaken.

Three points need to be made about donors' practices (or potential practices) in monitoring and evaluation. First, such work is clearly not a primary concern for donors, as evidenced by this type of work consistently missing from sector reform projects. Second, it is doubtful that donors wish to devote many resources to such work, although their program officers may be interested, both intellectually and as managers, in having the information. To be supported, monitoring and evaluation in sector reform projects must be low cost and efficient. Third, inclusion of such work in terms of reference and contracts is probably best handled as a block of resources to be used for these tasks.

Flexibility is key. The chief-of-party should have great latitude in committing modest resources to such activities. I emphasize "modest" because I am certainly not advocating the creeping transformation of action-oriented sector reform programs into research projects. To some degree, there will be a process of learning-by-doing to determine which investments produce the most serviceable results. Many program managers for bilateral and multilateral donors may be pleasantly surprised at the richness of the information generated, and its utility in discussions within their own agency and in multinational fora.

CASE: The assessment of the housing allowance program in the fall of 1994, done in response to concerns voiced by some national government and local administrators about low participation, was mounted in a matter of weeks. In late December 1995, the team was offered the chance to include questions in a national survey that would permit the first national estimate of the number of households participating in the housing allowance program. But the commitment had to be made within days because of the scheduled start of the field work on January 8. Because of the latitude in the contract, it was possible to take advantage of this offer, with the data delivered in March.[11]

Lesson: Monitoring and evaluation are important elements in a sector technical cooperation program because they provide the basis for rapid policy interventions and mid-course corrections in projects. They deserve more attention from the donors and implementers alike.

PROJECT COHERENCE

As noted in chapter 3, there are several ways to organize a sector reform program, with the simplest being the single donor–single contractor model. Even when a single donor is providing assistance to a sector in a particular country, the program managers shy away from hiring only a single contractor to execute the project. Rather, several contractors are typically hired to execute various parts of the program. Clearly, the multiple-contractor model carries the cost of having to coordinate activity among the teams, whereas with a single contractor working in a sector, intraprogram coordination will be relatively simple. In this section I argue that—even though there are many reasons why donors prefer multiple contractors—it is important for project success to keep the number down, preferably to one.

The principal rationale for hiring multiple contractors is to reduce risk to the donor. If there are multiple contractors and one fails to meet the objectives of its project, the program is damaged but not fatally flawed; the failure of a sole contractor of a project to perform well, however, is catastrophic.

Dividing a sector reform program among several contractors can also dramatically increase donor control. Multiple small projects, especially those with short time limits, make it easy for contract managers to keep contractors under constant pressure through the implicit threat of replacement. With small projects the manager receives more reports per dollar spent and can more easily be involved in the details of project management on the assumption the manager has the time to pursue all these reports. Seriously, in some projects, donor contract managers approve *every* person hired on the project—foreign or local, professional or support staff. Donor oversight is essential, but the wrong kind can clearly be debilitating to project performance.

Senior aid managers also argue that the trend to defining small, short projects (possibly within a broader overall sector reform project) is driven by the necessity to show quick results to donor countries' parliaments in order to justify continued budget support for a particular area of activity. Clearly, however, parsing the work program into pieces is inefficient from the perspective of both execution and management (much more paperwork and reports from a host of projects than one or two consolidated projects); and it militates against a comprehensive sector reform project being defined and implemented.

The difficulties of multi-contractor coordination can be illustrated with the following example. In the fall of 1995, the real estate reform program, within USAID Russia's privatization program, was a large and complicated operation. USAID had seven separate contracts in force covering these tasks:

- *Legislation*
  1. development of national legislation on land and real estate
- *Demonstration projects*
  2. real estate information systems
  3. enterprise land sales
  4. land use regulation
  5. property tax system development
  6. commercial real estate mortgage
- *Dissemination/transfer*
  7. training in real estate
  8. public education in land issues

The Housing Sector Reform Program, carrying out work, some of which was closely related to these topics, was in yet another part of the USAID portfolio.

CASE: USAID employed a senior American staffer and a couple of Russian assistants to oversee and coordinate the work in the real estate reform program. In addition, USAID contracted for another senior American with a Russian assistant. This team, located in the Russian Private Center (a nonprofit firm established to help implement the mass privatization program), was to coordinate parts of the overall program and to be the program's primary interface with the government, particularly the State Property Committee.[12]

Coordination met with only limited success. The individual contractors had narrow statements of work, with clearly stated performance indicators against which their results could be measured. Success in these narrow terms naturally came first in importance for them. The incentives for real cooperation were limited. Contractors want to win future contracts in the same field. They thereby wished to gain an advantage in future competitions by restricting the flow of information about their work. As stated previously, genuine monitoring reports detailing the developments in a sector are rare because contracts do not require them.

The coordination process was also flawed in more fundamental respects. Most contractors implementing demonstration projects with whom we spoke in 1995 did not see their task as reporting on their experience in implementation to the contractor charged with developing new laws in the real estate sector. Each successful project would have its own dissemination and "roll out" plan. One part of the overall program was a series of short newsletters prepared for public information on developments in the real estate sector that were designed in part to package information from all the relevant projects. But the newsletters were short on news from the demonstration projects.

After some months, during which the USAID program manager and the RPC coordinator attempted to work out coordination working bilaterally with each contractor, monthly contractor coordination meetings, chaired by the USAID program officer, were instituted in October 1995. But these were discontinued after six months. The difficulties of coordination of such a large number of projects, with the relevant government agencies, with AID staff, and among the assorted contractors, is a rigorous challenge even if adequate resources could be devoted to it. The difficulties in this case are attested to by the successive RPC American program coordinators quitting their job after relatively short periods of work. As the program matured over the next year and the number of projects shrank, the coordination problems diminished as well.

Coordination across multiple contractors is common to most sector reform programs. In Eastern Europe, USAID in the early 1990s contracted with three firms to work on housing sector reform. Each contract was for a separate substantive area (e.g., housing policy and finance, reform of the construction industry) and all contractors were to work in all countries. Later additional grants or contracts were awarded to provide help for development of the residential real estate sector and to strengthen reform in the construction sector. Coordination problems existed at two levels. Within each country waves of consultants arrived to work on housing sector reform with little knowledge of what others were doing and often meeting separately with the same host country officials. And the extent of information sharing among the contractors was extremely limited. In any event, this very difficult situation was mitigated in a few countries by the resident advisor acting as the traffic cop and keeping order. Where there was no one to play this role, there was great confusion and waste. In the follow-up round of contracting, USAID decided to abandon the three-contractor model and to contract with a single prime contractor that would provide some coordination as a matter of course. There is still the challenge of coordination among workers of the prime contractors and several subcontractors. But at least the new arrangement fixes the responsibility for coordination.

The problems just described are substantially compounded where multiple donors as well as multiple contractors are involved, unless there is a clear lead donor who takes meaningful responsibility for coordination. Known examples of successful coordination on this model involve the World Bank as the lead donor, with the Bank taking the overall lead in appraising and funding a sector loan. Then other donors contribute cash or in-kind services at the design stage and funding or direct provision of technical cooperation during implementation. However, these projects are seldom full sector reform projects, containing all five elements stated in chapter 1. The emphasis, rather, is on demonstrations involving projects requiring substantial capital finance.[13]

CASE: USAID, perhaps to minimize the risk of total project failure, decided to issue two contracts for housing sector reform in the Russian Federation, making the HSRP a two-contractor model. The contractors were not charged with different tasks to be operated throughout the country. Rather, they were charged with the same tasks but in different parts of the country. The Urban Institute was assigned to Central Russia, including Moscow and St. Petersburg. The second contractor, PADCO, was assigned to work in the Urals region and Siberia, with initial work concentrated in the cities of Ekaterinburg and Novosibirsk. The two projects developed in different ways and there was very limited coordination between them, which produced significant duplication, even though they concentrated in different regions. USAID chaired the first formal coordination meeting in October 1995—three years after the contracts were signed. The principal overlaps were in the creation of condominium associations and holding competitions among firms for contracts to maintain municipal housing. Both teams developed their own training materials and information brochures for local government and new associations. After October 1995 sharing of materials between the two increased markedly.

Lesson: The fewer separate contracts or separate projects in a sector reform technical cooperation program, the easier will be intraprogram coordination and the greater the efficiency of the overall program. The need to show results quickly can be addressed by proper program phasing, as indicated in an earlier lesson about concentrating early in a project on a few tasks, and through a strong monitoring component, which will generate hard information on project accomplishments.

The donor community should take this lesson to heart, since donor agencies are often understaffed and find full coordination among separate projects extremely demanding. The tactic of dividing work among multiple contractors as a form of risk reduction is questionable. More consistent and more intense oversight of one or two contractors may be more effective in preventing project failures than many contractors working with only general oversight.

CONTINUITY IN IMPLEMENTATION

Problems of continuity among expatriate advisors during the implementation stage of a technical cooperation project take two forms: overly short contract periods and poorly prepared consultants. Each can have serious adverse consequences.

The first is a problem of the donors' own making, arising from contracting for periods as brief as six to eight months. At the end of each work period, the donor has three options: (1) in the case of high quality performance, extend the contract for a new stage of the project; (2) for a less successful project that needs more time to complete the current phase, extend the contract for more effort on that phase; and (3) in the case of poor performance, terminate the contract. In the last case, the donor must then decide whether to continue the project; if the answer is "yes," another contractor is hired, possibly through a new competition.

Contractors—both firms and individuals—find this type of arrangement singularly unattractive because all the risk of project problems falls on them. There are many potential sources of problems in a project, only some of which are the fault of the contractor. Yet the contractor may well pay the full price of failure. In addition, if firms are required to mobilize teams of expatriate consultants quickly but are unable to offer team members any assurance of work beyond the initial period, many of the better freelance consultants will refuse such an assignment because of the short initial period. This is a rational response. While they are on assignment out of their home country, it is relatively difficult to hunt for new assignments, which means they are likely to face several months of unemployment before the next job. Obviously, they would rather have a longer period of assured employment between payless spells.

The inherent problems of this "roll-over" model are aggravated by the donors making decisions about whether to extend the contract very late in the initial contract period. Even if the decision is made to extend, there is a good chance that some team members will move on to new jobs they have already accepted in order to protect themselves from being unemployed. A new consultant has to be recruited immediately and dispatched to the country. Clearly, there are very substantial costs to the project in such a pattern. Experienced professionals, who have become oriented to the project at substantial expense, are lost. The rush to find a replacement nearly always means that a less than ideal candidate is found. Host country clients are also vexed by having to "break in" another expatriate advisor.

USAID's omnibus contracts provide the agency maximum contracting freedom. The type of roll over problem just described was endemic in the use of contracts in the real estate reform part of the Russian privatization program listed earlier. Contractors complained about the cost of working under such uncertainty and about the loss of seasoned consultants as a result. The problem is especially acute when the initial task order (contract) is written with goals that are overly ambitious for the initial contract period. Clearly, the contractor is merely being tested; if the firm makes reasonable progress during the initial period, the contract will be extended. Meanwhile, team members are spending valuable time looking for new jobs, since the decision to extend can be rather arbitrary. Extension, in other words, depends on the program officer's judgment about "reasonable progress" in a situation where the scope of work is unrealistic and the real goals of the initial period unclear.

Rethinking the utility of such contracting methods is in order. The costs associated with excessive staff turnover and operating under uncertainty are extreme.

Inadequate briefing is a continuity problem created by the contractor—successive waves of short-term consultants being inadequately briefed by the contractor on developments in the sector and the project before meeting with host country officials or service providers. These officials understandably become irritated with the task of explaining the basics to a constant succession of fresh consultants. I have heard numerous complaints from officials in cities selected to be included in a World Bank loan about the waves of poorly prepared consultants who visited their cities during the loan's extensive appraisal phase.

Information provided to prior visitors had simply not been shared with others in the project team. This problem is not endemic to World Bank projects, of course, but is not an isolated event either. Obviously, the problem here is one of enormous waste of scarce resources: the time of highly skilled consultants, officials, and service providers with more work than they can do in a day even in the absence of foreign visitors.

The best defense is twofold. First, minimize the number of new short-term consultants used. Second, make sure the resident team has explicit responsibility for thoroughly briefing newcomers and narrowly targeting meetings with local officials and other counterparts.

Lesson: Donors should avoid organizing projects as a sequential set of short-term contracts (six to nine months) in order to maximize control over the project. They run the grave risk of substantial turnover in resident foreign consultants and enormous resource costs as a result. Contractors should have as a constant goal to minimize the number of short-term advisors on a project. Where new advisors must be introduced, before meeting with local counterparts, they should be made thoroughly knowledgeable, not only about the project but also about conditions in the country.

Notes

1. I do not discuss explicitly such basic aspects of project implementation and oversight as the timely preparation of work plans by contractors and their review and approval by donors, the submission of progress reports by contractors, and the routine oversight of contractor performance by the donors. According to GAO (1995b), all seven donors they reviewed (exclusive of USAID) had trouble in these areas. In general, as the use of contractors to implement projects has increased, the greater have become the difficulties of monitoring. USAID's Regional Inspector General also criticizes USAID managers for their performance in these areas (Competellor, 1995).

Nor do I discuss effective dissemination techniques, in the sense of distributing printed reports, participation in sponsoring conferences, seminars, and training courses. My sense is that the context is so important for determining what will be effective that there are no general lessons. In the next chapter I do present a series of lessons about project dissemination in the sense of replicating the successful results of pilot projects.

2. Layard and Parker (1996: 299) make a similar point in their broad assessment of Russian reform:

> In general the technical assistance has been poorly administered. There has inevitably been much muddle at the Russian end, but things have been scarcely better at the Western end. The West should have realized that to be effective in Russia its technical assistance programs needed to be run from Moscow. Instead the Western

agencies operated the traditional "mission" system, where teams make short visits often followed by other teams, which repeat the same questions. Thus much time and money have been wasted. But some results of extreme worth have been achieved. USAID is an important exception to the pattern described: it both established a sizable presence in Russia to manage the U.S. bilateral program and generally emphasized resident advisors in its projects.
For further description and critique of the initial approach, see GAO (1991a, b and 1992).

3. Based on the following salaries, inclusive of income taxes: Russian staffer, $2,500 per month; U.S. staffer, $4,175 ($50,000 per year).

4. Not surprisingly, businessmen working in the region also favor giving responsibility to local staff. See, for example, Lawrence and Vlachoutsicous (1993).

5. Institutional Reform and the Informal Sector, a program of the Department of Economics of the University of Maryland.

6. J. Keay, "Consultants in Eastern Europe Say They Aren't to Blame for Projects' Failures," *International Herald Tribune*, October 16, 1995, p. 11.

7. Buyck (1991: vii) also notes the lack of creativity in exploiting the resources of local professionals in technical cooperation projects in World Bank–supported projects in developing countries.

8. Monitoring of project achievements is a different topic. This is a whole process of establishing indicators, usually quantitative, to measure whether the project achieves its explicitly stated objectives. Obviously, the contractor is required to gather the data to construct the performance indicators. Such indicators are now commonly employed by the donors. Typically, the indicators are written into the contract itself, i.e., they are defined before the launching of field implementation. Donor agencies rely heavily on these in their project assessments and reporting. A description of the logic behind and the definition of performance indicators is given in World Bank (1996).

9. The information campaigns are only one element in increasing participation rates. The increase in rents raised the benefits from participation and this was clearly an important factor.

10. An overview of this project is in Annex B. The information cited in the text is from Abt Associates (1995).

11. The survey was the fifth round of the "New Russian Barometer" organized by Professor Richard Rose.

12. USAID use of contractors to coordinate programs is not exceptional. For example, in Russia the firm CH2M Hill coordinates the environmental programs.

13. These projects usually have a policy reform component, which is stressed to varying degrees in execution. They tend to be thin on monitoring and evaluation, dissemination, and institutionalization beyond their work with the executing government agency.

14. There is another little-used element in a sector reform cooperation program that I do not discuss in the text. It is to make small grants directly to implementing agencies to encourage their participation in the program. The USAID-Russia health sector reform program (see Annex B) included a substantial ($3 million) grant program of this type. Grants went to a variety of participants. Hospitals received grants to initiate new services or to upgrade information and management systems. Cities received grants to conduct information campaigns on personal health, disease, and outbreak prevention and over-the-counter medication. Grants were significant, many being in the $50,000 to $100,000 range. The grants were made mostly on a competitive basis, through an RFP process. Different competitions were aimed at different groups broadly involved in the provision of health care. For example, one round was directed at cities for a

"healthy cities" program. In this case the RFP was distributed at a meeting sponsored by the health section of the Russian Union of Cities.

The project's chief-of-party argues the program was highly effective. First, the program certainly attracts attention to the reform program. Those interested in the competitions are exposed to the program's objectives and operations through studying the materials in the grant package. Second, it fosters commitment to the reform because grantees implement reforms of their own conception—not those pressed on them from the outside. Sustainability is likely increased. Third, it is efficient: administrative costs were estimated to be equivalent to about 15 percent of grants awarded.

The Local Government Initiative in Bulgaria provided each of the 10 demonstration municipalities with $50,000 in grant funds, which could be used for project-related expenses such as the purchase of computers and other equipment or renovation of space for a newly created economic development NGO. In the project manager's opinion, the grant funds were not critical in securing the participation of municipalities in the project. The grants did, however, result in significantly greater attention being given to the project by the mayor and other senior officials.

While the experience with grants as part of this program appears highly positive, I have too little exposure to other projects using this format—projects in this region or elsewhere—to feel confident in using a grant program as a "lesson" for other projects.

Chapter Six

BEYOND DEMONSTRATIONS

Few projects actually reach the "mass replication stage." Donor frustrations with the difficulties of successfully replicating pilot projects, (i.e., making them an active part of the country's policy) are well known.[1] The reasons are multiple, but four stand out:

- the pilot project is not successful, and therefore should not be replicated;
- the pilot is successful but the donor loses interest, perhaps believing that a concluding conference or report on the demonstration is sufficient for the widespread adoption of the innovation (in rare cases it is);
- local opposition to the change, which was passive during the pilot stage, becomes active when threatened with broader implementation and blocks expansion;
- the project fails to motivate other cities, banks, or organizations sufficiently to adopt the innovation.

The rewards of replication can be substantial, nonetheless. Even if the expanded programs do not blanket the country in the near term, they may succeed in gaining such widespread acceptance for the innovation that they make the innovation irreversible.

Examples in the former Soviet bloc of "roll out," to use the term now in fashion, have been much noted.[2] These can be merely the addition of one or two more pilot sites, with little systemic change. But they can also signal genuine institutionalization.

CASE: USAID's Enterprise Land Sales project, which assists local governments in establishing procedures for selling land controlled by enterprises but still owned by the municipality to the enterprise, is an example from Russia. A 1994 Presidential Decree made such sales possible. Secure ownership of the land eliminates the risk to the enterprise of losing control of it. In addition, land in excess of that currently being used by the enterprise is often a valuable asset that could be sold to raise cash. After a successful pilot effort in several cities in early 1995, assistance was provided to over 30 cities in 1995–1996. Most municipalities like it because it raises badly needed funds. Enterprises want to purchase their plots to eliminate any future challenge to their control of the site and to gain a valuable asset at a reasonable price. The only opponents to the program are against any sale of land to private entities, on principle.

GET THE INCENTIVES RIGHT

Projects selected for mass replication are unlikely to be successful unless local governments, banks, or others recognize the benefits for themselves of undertaking them. The incentives in the Enterprise Land Sales project are clear. Examples are also available from the HSRP.

CASE: Residents of a building who have privatized their units and created an association have the right to take over management of the building from the state firm heretofore responsible for its maintenance. The building receives the operating subsidies, which previously went to the state firm to cover the cost of providing services to the building not defrayed by tenant payments. Thus, the tenants are able to select and control their own management firm or to self-manage and hire a maintenance firm. In either case, conditions in the building are very likely to improve. The municipality for its part benefits from condominiums being formed because it is no longer responsible for their maintenance. It must continue to pay operating subsidies in the short term, but these are scheduled to be phased out nationally by 2003. The only opposition comes from municipal maintenance departments, because they lose revenue when management responsibility shifts.

CASE: Banks are profit motivated and their principal interest in beginning long-term housing lending is to increase profits over the long term. Starting early (i.e., before the mortgage lending system is fully developed) gives them market position for when the system works more smoothly. In Russia's rough and tumble financial markets, multiyear lending to families for unit purchase carries moderate risk compared with the alternative—lending to enterprises and to other banks in the large interbank market. Underwriting tends to be rigorous and interest rates competitive with other lending. Under these conditions a significant number of banks, including some of the country's largest banks, have begun limited long-term lending for home purchase.[3]

The lack of proper incentives is usually crippling.

CASE: The HSRP initiated a pilot project for allocating municipal land for residential development purposes through a tender process in two cities, Tver and Nizhni Novgorod. Under the Soviet system, land was allocated to those who needed it without payment. During the transition land allocation has continued under lease rights or use rights, with payment to local government usually being in the form of fees for infrastructure or in-kind payments as a percentage of the housing units built. Under the pilot project the necessary changes were made in local laws and regulations and the bidding process was carried out on several plots. But none of the auctions was successful. In part this was because local developers already controlled, formally or informally, sufficient land to meet their near-term needs. But it was also because the existing informal, opaque process was advantageous to both the local officials and developers. The incentives in this case were in the wrong direction. Implementation of an open auction process is probably a few years in the future.[4]

Lesson: In considering whether a pilot project can be replicated on a significant scale, check to be certain that the incentives to key actors—local officials and/or service providers—to carry out the reform are in fact positive and perceived clearly.

SHIFT TO A "DEMAND-DRIVEN" APPROACH

It is generally difficult to find a local government, bank, or other organization that wants to be the first to introduce an innovation. Hence, technical assistance teams must work hard at convincing the innovator of the virtues of the new approach when it has to be done in the abstract. However, once a pilot project has been successfully implemented and documented, the need for the hard sell will steadily diminish. Indeed, if properly marketed, demand for the innovation will increase.

The HSRP marketed its success stories energetically, in the press, through its own publication of evaluation results and guide books for conducting the pilot project, and through many, many presentations.

CASE: A key vehicle for dissemination was the production of "brochures," papers or reports offset-printed in a book-size format. Printed in Moscow, these could be produced for under 50 cents a copy. In the first three-and-a-half years of the project, about 200,000 such documents were distributed, mainly at conferences, seminars, and training courses in which the HSRP team were presenters. Copies were also made available for distribution to the Union of Russian Cities and other trade associations. A few were adopted as official guidance by the Ministry of Construction and distributed by the Ministry to regional and local administrations nationwide. The housing finance team developed the "Mortgage Handbook Series" that is sold commercially and is also distributed as part of the materials for mortgage lending training courses.

Additionally, the team was receptive to visits from city officials and bankers visiting Moscow on other business. Often these were literally "drop ins," people arriving without prior warning. At a minimum short discussions were fit in and a full set of materials provided. When advanced arrangements could be made, the team would make a program for visitors lasting from a half day to a week. In one case, for example, team members in Vladivostok for a finance conference met with the deputy mayor, who requested intensive help with reforming his maintenance operations. The team arranged a one-week tutorial for the department head in Moscow a couple of weeks later—which coincided with a visit for another purpose. Vladivostok was never intended to be a site where the Urban Institute worked because of its distance from Moscow, but this kind of cooperation was important in increasing awareness of reforms.

Through the printed documents, press stories, Moscow-based meetings and tutorials, and presentations at conferences, seminars and training courses, the project became well known in the country at large, which gave team members entree and credibility in approaching new clients. As a result of the promotion drive, shortly after the team began to offer to work with other cities and additional banks to introduce an innovation it began receiving requests for help.

When a program graduates to a demand-driven mode, it is possible to deploy the technical assistance team very flexibly, working with numerous clients at the same time, with each client advancing at its own pace. If one city is not ready for the next step (because, for example, it has difficulty passing the necessary legislation), the team works with others. This permits a highly efficient use of the implementing team's resources.

Lesson: Do not force-feed assistance in the roll-out phase. Offer assistance to a large group of clients and work more or less intensively with each in accordance with the interest each exhibits.

ORGANIZE TO WORK AT THE WHOLESALE LEVEL

As the project shifts from implementing a limited demonstration to operating at numerous sites, the "production function" should change quite dramatically. Two dimensions of change stand out.

First, the intensive teaching and mentoring of clients characteristic of the demonstration phase should be replaced with a combination of structured courses taught at a central or regional facility and only a modest amount of "hands-on" assistance. The courses can be offered as frequently as necessary and can serve the needs of all the cities with which the project is working.[5] In some cases only one or two offerings of the courses or conferences will be needed; in others repetition may continue for several years. In any case the use of courses permits the level of on-site assistance to be sharply reduced compared with the pilot project.

Second, the size and composition of the technical assistance team should change from a couple of senior experts during the demonstration phase to a larger number of mid-level experts trained by the technical assistance team to provide help to cities on a particular topic. These experts provide the hands-on assistance required after local officials have attended the relevant course.

CASE: In the HSRP, the project's "regional team" grew rapidly from five to fourteen professionals when the tasks assigned to it shifted. The first stage involved working with a few cities to create the first condominium associations and to hold the first competitions for selecting maintenance firms. The second stage was working with more cities, pushing for a maximum volume in condominium creation, and having buildings maintained by competitively selected firms.

There are six basic models for providing on-site assistance:

1. Station an expatriate advisor with the client, possibly as the head of a team with local professionals.
2. Station one local professional or a team on site.
3. Station a local professional or team on site and supplement their work with visits by a more senior person (expatriate or local).
4. Hire a local institution, whose staff is trained by the team, to work with the client.
5. Hire a local institution to work with the client and supplement their work with visits by a more senior person.
6. Use site visits by experts from a centrally located team.

All but #6 carry the risk of having more resources on site than can be absorbed and thus incurring the cost of unused resources. Option #6, however, can result in underservicing the client ("client neglect"), with attendant loss of interest or at least slower progress on implementation than could otherwise be the case.

The choice among these models depends on the complexity of the task, the intensity with which assistance should be provided, and the absorptive capacity of the recipient. The capacity of the assistance provider is also a factor.

Choosing the intensity of assistance provision appropriate to any particular task requires a delicate combination of deliberation and judgment. On the one hand, lots of help to the client (say, the local government) should accelerate the pace of reform. On the other hand, the more the client organization does for itself, the more deeply it is likely to be committed to the changes. There can be too much help. Giving the local government the lead on drafting its new regulations (while providing model documents, giving guidance, and responding to questions) is better than simply taking the lead. Similarly, banks need a business plan to guide their mortgage lending operations. When the bankers take primary responsibility for preparing the plan, they are more likely to defend it ably to the board of management than if the consultant prepares it using information provided by the bankers.

Absorptive capacity has two dimensions in the former Soviet bloc. The one that is traditionally referred to in the technical cooperation projects has to do with recipient capability: the rate at which new ideas can be mastered and actions required for implementing them organized by the recipient. The second has to do with recipient capacity: the amount of time and resources the recipient will devote to the project. One must recognize that the recipients have other responsibilities and time-sensitive tasks. For local government administrators, for example, meeting the demands of the budget cycle is an absolute requirement. Dealing with crises is mandatory—an example here is a burst district heating pipe in the dead of the Russian winter. For bankers, closing the books at the end of the fiscal year is a clear imperative.

The traditional definition of absorptive capacity only implicitly accounts for the "level of *possible* effort" the client can devote to the accepting and implementing innovation. Paying explicit attention as well to the level of plausible effort is very important in determining how much technical assistance resources to devote to clients per unit of time. Not only does pushing too much help at a client too fast often result in the technical cooperation team taking over responsibilities that should belong to the recipient. It may also cause the recipient to lose interest because the cost of participating is too high—in terms of the opportunity cost of the regular responsibilities for which he is really accountable.

CASE: The HSRP has used different models to fit alternative circumstances. The early experience with banks showed that the leadership and staff in the credit department could not spend more than parts of two days at a time at their bank meeting with an assistance team. The bank staff did their homework between visits, however, so the start-up of long-term housing lending typically went fairly quickly. In this case model #6 was clearly right.

A similar arrangement was used in working with cities to draft, pass, and implement local regulations for the creation of condominium associations. Episodic visits by centrally based team members, supplemented with various materials and phone calls, proved sufficient for cities that were truly interested in this innovation. The project's objective was to get condominiums formed in a critical mass of cities as quickly as possible. Cities reluctant or uninterested a few months before became more interested in the innovation as it became more commonplace and administrators better understood the advantages to the city.

CASE: The Russian Privatization Center (RPC), which had also decided to work with cities on creating condominiums, chose a different model—model #2. Beginning in early 1995, the RPC initially worked in two locations, Tumen *Oblast* and St. Petersburg. A four-person RPC team of Russian professionals, including a lawyer, was dispatched to be resident in each site. The teams had the advantage of various documents already available but had very little practical experience on this topic. By the summer of 1995, the teams had been working in the two locations for several months with little visible results. However, by April 1996 the St. Petersburg team—now augmented to a staff of 20—had worked with 31 buildings to form condominium associations. By Russian standards of the time this was a large number of new condominiums. My own view is that in this case model #6 would have been better until the initial work with the local government was complete; then shifting to the more resource-intensive model #2 would have made sense.

CASE: A 1995 USAID/Russia contract to promote commercial bank lending for real estate projects other than mortgage finance directed the consultant firm, the Barents Group, to identify two banks that would agree to initiate such lending and to place a full-time expatriate advisor in each bank (model #1). After the team had worked for two months on refining the project design and identifying banks, the limited absorptive capacity of banks was recognized and the decision made to work more flexibly with more banks (model #6) rather than bank-based advisors.

CASE: The HSRP used model #3 in five cities as part of its Enterprise Housing Divestiture work. In the Soviet era, enterprises provided more housing than municipalities—about 40 percent of all units nationwide. The broad goal of the project is to encourage enterprises to transfer their housing to municipalities, so that senior management can concentrate on restructuring the firm to compete in the world economy. After initial resistance, a very large number of enterprises transferred or were willing to transfer their housing. The problem became municipalities' financial ability to absorb the new housing. Part of the solution is to increase the efficiency with which housing maintenance and management is carried out. The World Bank, with help from USAID, is piloting a project to assist cities with these responsibilities. The Urban Institute is providing technical assistance to five of these cities. The plan calls for (1) a rapid shift of maintenance operations from state monopolist firms to firms selected through competition and (2) a strong effort to encourage the formation of condominium associations to take care of management responsibilities in their buildings. Hiring a housing professional, resident in each city, to work full time on the project was deemed essential, at least in the first year. The efforts of the residents were augmented by frequent visits from the core project staff. The residents also participate in regular training and problem solving seminars in Moscow that involve the whole project team.

CASE: Under a contract with USAID/Russia, and on the basis of field reconnaissance, the Cooperative Housing Foundation placed a U.S. resident advisor in the city of Tver in the summer of 1995 to develop a lending program for rehabilitation of apartment buildings where condominium associations had formed. It quickly became clear that local banks were not interested in such lending. Collateralized lending in general was new and there were severe credit risk issues involved in using owner-occupied housing as loan collateral. In addition, there were very few condominiums in the city and the Soviet era cooperatives did not turn out to be ready to consider such borrowing. While the resident advisor shifted his focus to helping form more condominium associations and an "association of associations," including housing coops, he was clearly underutilized until an augmented assignment was defined. In this case a model in which the consultant was not wed to a single site would have been superior.

Lesson: Station people full time at a client's location—be it a bank, an enterprise, or a municipal government—only after fully satisfying oneself that alternative arrangements will not be adequate to provide intensive enough assistance. The risk of underutilized resources is too great. Centrally based mobile teams will often be the superior option for delivering advice.

KNOW WHEN TO STOP

As gratifying as it is for both donor and technical cooperation team to remain around to see continued progress on the ground, they must determine the point at which outside help is no longer needed to sustain progress. In some cases a phased exit may be wise, in others simply letting go is appropriate. The key indicator for the decision to terminate "roll-out" activities is the number of cities, banks, or enterprises that are adopting the particular innovation as a significant part of their regular operations. A "critical mass" stage has to be reached. A bank may begin long-term housing lending by making a handful of loans to bank staff or favored clients; the loans might even be at subsidized interest rates. While this is a step in the right direction,

such lending clearly has a special status. The bank needs to be orig-
inating 10 to 15 loans a month to the general public, or to employees
of an enterprise that has agreed to take some of the credit risk. Projects
that have set up good sector monitoring systems will be in a much
better position to determine when an innovation has reached the critical mass stage.

CASE: In the HSRP the first demonstration project was the introduction of housing maintenance services provided by firms selected
through competition. The first contracts were signed in March 1993.
While there were more competitions in the next year, there were
difficulties in the spring of 1994, and the project team remained
fully involved. But by early 1995, with about 150,000 units under
contract to private firms, the demonstration had taken off. District
administrations were holding competitions without project assistance and the course on how to conduct such competitions and to
manage the contractors was being regularly offered on a fee basis.
The project team turned to other work and only responded to requests for specific help. By December 1995, 325,000 units were in
the program, about 15 percent of the municipal housing inventory.

CASE: In September 1996 the HSRP was scheduled to stop working
with individual banks to initiate mortgage lending programs of
home purchase (with the exception of banks in two new regional
centers). By then, HSRP had assisted 30 banks to begin such lending
operations. To sustain the availability of services, the Institute for
Urban Economics, a new Russian institution, will consult with
banks on a commercial (i.e., a fee) basis.

Notes

1. See, for example, Cohen (1983) on the difficulties of getting the World Bank's sites-
and-services housing approach to move beyond the demonstration phase.

2. It is important to distinguish between replication of an innovative practice as part
of a sector reform project and ongoing assistance in carrying out a reform. An example
of the latter has been the very substantial assistance provided to agencies in many
countries responsible for industrial privatization. In a sense, the expatriate teams have
supplemented local staff in executing the program, rather than introducing some key
technology or helping establish the ground rules.

3. The somewhat awkward expression, "multiyear lending for home purchase," is used instead of the more standard, "mortgage lending," because most of this type of lending is not done using a true mortgage. The difficulties of evicting in case of default make most banks wary of such contracts. Rather, they are using a lease-purchase agreement under which the borrower has only a lease hold right to the unit being purchased (renewed monthly) until the loan is paid off. For details see Kosareva et al. (1996).

4. For more on the land auctions, see Butler et al. (1996). Interestingly, Moscow has been successful in allocating land for commercial projects through a tender process. The city, however, chose a somewhat different approach in that it first selected (through competition) four realty firms to be its agents in conducting tenders. The realty firms receive a commission. It may be that the firms conducting the auctions have maintained rewards to the local Land Committee and Chief Architect's office of the old system. Also important is that the city has sharply restricted the allocation of sites through noncompetitive means, thereby channeling demand to the competitive process. Several cities in the Ukraine have also conducted successful land auction, but the differences in the situation there and in Russian cities are not clear.

5. Organizing training courses is discussed in chapter 7.

EXIT STRATEGY AND BEYOND

INSTITUTIONALIZING REFORM

The goal of all sector reform technical cooperation projects is to see reforms through to such an extent that the outside advice and assistance is no longer needed. Seldom are projects extended to that point. The question then becomes, how can the project establish a local capacity that can take over its role in continuing to promote reform? This is a crucial task. I have referred often to the need to institutionalize reform. In this chapter I address how that final task can be accomplished.

The first, and most fundamental, step is to develop an "exit strategy." This is *not* a plan developed in the last months of a project to facilitate an orderly process for winding things up. It is a plan that should be developed *in the early months of the project*. Its purpose is to spell out specific goals which, if achieved, will lead to the sustaining of reforms once the external (donor) resources are withdrawn. Working toward the sustaining activities specified in the exit strategy should be a constant task throughout the project.

The task of institutionalization (and the exit strategy) is to create organizations and motivate them and individuals within the country to continue to pursue sector reforms. Institutionalization takes many forms: individual policy analysts, research and policy institutes, competent consulting firms, training programs, government policy offices, professional and trade associations, and other NGOs continuing to work for positive change. Many are private entities, some are government.[1] If institutionalization is successful, these entities, acting in their own self-interest, will continue the process of sector reform. This chapter discusses three major methods of institutionalization—augmenting training capacity, developing a cadre of professionals to continue the work of reform, and creating or strengthening technical and professional associations.

AUGMENTING TRAINING CAPACITY

The term training carries many different meanings depending on the audience. In the context of sector reform it is useful to distinguish among at least six different types of activity:

(1) Development and offering of formal courses that provide in-depth coverage of a topic. Such courses are generally repeated periodically. Development includes preparation of instructor's guides to preserve course quality and content as additional instructors and institutions offer the course. Producing these courses requires substantial resources. A key part of the program is training local professionals to offer the course independently and motivating local institutions to offer the course without continuing financial assistance from the project.

(2) One-time conferences, typically on a regional or national basis, that serve to inform participants about several topics less intensively than the courses. These are best done with cooperating local institutions. Compared with courses they involve relatively little effort.

(3) One-day or half-day seminars offered by implementation teams as part of a project. These are geared to informing and motivating implementers—local officials, bankers, hospital administrators, or others—in the early stages of introducing an innovation in a city or region.

(4) In-country study tours, which bring administrators, developers, or bankers from various regions to a particular site to observe an innovative practice and talk with the innovators in a structured way. As acceptance of the general idea grows within the country, these visits are less necessary.

(5) "Elite conferences," where experts meet and exchange notes, receive information on new legal developments, and discuss ideas for new innovations.

(6) Study tours to Western countries, where new practices are seen firsthand. These can be an invaluable complement to more abstract planning for change.

Each of these training vehicles has its advantages in certain circumstances. Often project leaders do not make a conscious decision about which vehicles to employ or when one vehicle is likely to be most effective.[2] Many simply assume that the combination of a foreigner-taught workshop or two and the study tour to the West is the way to proceed, in part because of the popularity of the latter with clients. This is misguided. The mix of training activities and how they are organized have a strong impact on the development of training capacity.

At one end of the spectrum of in-country training is the quite typical practice of a contractor bringing in expatriate experts to teach a course. A local institution may handle the logistics, but the teaching is by outsiders. No attempt is made to work with local trainers. Where the topic is brand new, this may be unavoidable for a first course offering; but repeated offerings in this format are particularly inefficient. They do not help build local capacity and they are very expensive.

Development of training capacity has three distinct aspects: creation of material with a rigorous technical content fully adapted to the local situation to be presented (and the accompanying instructor's guides), training of trainers in stimulating teaching techniques, and development of a strong financial basis for offering the courses. The extent of investment in a particular course is an important matter of judgment. During the transition, for example, much of the need for instruction is of a passing nature.

CASE: One aspect of the HSRP was to work with local governments to create condominiums. Assistance to local government was critical for two reasons. Under the initial Federal legislation (actually a Presidential Decree), certain local legal acts were prerequisites. In addition, local governments had to agree to continue the building-specific subsidies during the transition period, or else there would be little incentive for tenants to form the condominium associations. For some months a course on the condominium concept and the contents of the necessary legal acts (including distribution of model laws) proved highly popular. Demand then dried up. Cities had mastered this part of reform. In this instance, training capacity was developed by having Russians do most of the teaching. The decision was made not to develop a detailed instructor's guide.

CASE: A course for bankers on mortgage loan origination and servicing was deemed by the HSRP to have a lasting audience in the form of staff at new banks beginning mortgage loans and successive waves of new staff in the mortgage loan departments of experienced banks. Therefore a comprehensive instructor's guide and course materials were developed for four separate courses on loan origination and servicing, and on pricing (setting the interest rate charged) and managing the financial risk in such lending.

Lesson: Instructor's guides and in-depth training for trainers on a particular subject are warranted only for courses for which there will likely be a lasting demand.

An obvious element in building the capacity of training institutes and upgrading the technical quality of the courses offered is for firms implementing sector reform projects to make it a rule to co-sponsor and co-teach with local institutions. Co-sponsoring, in particular, gives one a strong voice in setting the agenda and in controlling quality.

Perhaps the greatest challenge in designing a strategy for institutionalizing training is to balance the supply of training with probable demand. Stated simply, there will be some types of training for which there will be adequate demand in every large city. For more specialized training, e.g., mortgage banking, demand is likely to be sufficient only to support national level institutions, and perhaps only one such entity until the number of banks making mortgage loans expands into the dozens from the few banks doing so in the early years of reform. Creating training capacity where there is insufficient demand will be wasteful of project funds and could well produce resentment at the local level when the project cannot help the training programs survive.

The sense of the HSRP in 1995 was that the appropriate distribution of formal training programs, given the perceived demand for training in different topics, was something like the following:

Local

- Condominium boards on establishing and running associations
- Property management for condominium associations

Regional

- City officials on conducting competitions to select private maintenance firms
- Infrastructure pricing for local officials, developers, and utility companies

National

- For local officials on the creation of the necessary legal and regulatory framework for condominium associations
- Housing management—with some regional offerings

- Mortgage and construction finance courses—with some regional offerings of the courses
- Infrastructure finance
- Urban land auctions and zoning—with some regional offerings of the courses

In some cases, several distinct courses would be offered for a given topic. For example, the Association of Mortgage Banks working with the Urban Institute offered four separate courses.

In every instance these courses were offered by Russian institutions. The Urban Institute had to identify appropriate partners at the local, regional, and national levels. The courses were based on materials developed by the U.S. experts and modified by Russian staff to fit the Russian reality. They were at least initially taught by joint teams of experts from the project team and instructors from the "host institute." Later the course was to be taken over by the host institute. The institute decides whether to develop its own faculty or to recruit teachers from other institutes, which have the necessary experts but do not have a separate education function. (In Russia, a special license is required to offer training courses.)

Lesson 1: Identify appropriate institutions, including trade associations and training institutes, with whom to jointly offer courses and seminars.

Lesson 2: Substitute local for foreign instructors quickly, even if it means extra expatriate training of trainers in the first offerings.

Lesson 3: Do not over-supply the market.

It is also important for the courses to meet the market test. If the courses are not profitable, they will not be taught when donor subsidies are withdrawn. Also, and more fundamentally, if the courses can only be taught with large subsidies, there is a problem with the basic training strategy for the reform in question. "Host institutes" should be selected in part based on their intrinsic interest in the subject, e.g., the Association of Mortgage Banks for housing finance. The greater their basic interest, the greater efforts they will extend to make the course a success in order to serve their constituency well. Some projects in the region have followed this approach. One example is the successful training activities of the Polish Foundation in Support of Local Democracy.

Occasional exceptions to the market-test rule need to be kept in mind, however. In the initial phases of reform implementation, subsidies are appropriate because it is imperative to inform critical actors about the innovations. At this stage those who the reformers most want to reach are unlikely to pay to be educated. It is also improbable that they will attend a several-day course. In this instance, half-day or full-day seminars or a block of time at a conference on a related topic are more appropriate vehicles. Once demand has been kindled through seminars, publications, and other vehicles, then fees sufficient to cover costs can be charged for follow-on courses. Subsidies to an institution may also be necessary when a whole new set of courses is to be offered.

Subsidies, when indicated, can take several forms. Most commonly, the institution is given training materials or very substantial assistance in preparing them and the teaching services of expatriate advisors is provided free of charge. Other options include grants of equipment, such as personal computers and a copy machine; paying the salaries of one or two staff members; and direct cash support. Wherever support is provided, it is important that there be a clear understanding that the assistance will be phased out and the time of the commitment made clear. This will spur the training institute to become self-sustaining.

CASE: In the HSRP training courses were offered only on a fee basis and with partner institutes. Similarly, the project frequently would provide a day's program at a larger conference for which attendees paid a fee. (Shorter seminars were generally presented without a fee.) Fees were set at levels comparable to other courses aimed at the same audience, e.g., bankers or city officials. These courses were subsidized by HSRP by making available Russian and some U.S. trainers at no cost. However, after a couple of years, the project began charging fees for its teachers similar to those typically paid thereby removing the subsidy and making the courses fully meet the market test.

Despite the promise of working with associations, institutes, and training organizations to build their own capacity, the great majority of donor seminars, workshops, and conferences are not used for this purpose. This may be appropriate in short-lived projects, but it is a valuable opportunity in most sector reform technical cooperation projects that should not be lost.

DEVELOPING LOCAL REFORM CAPACITY

One can identify three alternative working arrangements for the policy analysts, program designers, and consultants who will work with local governments, banks, hospitals, and other entities leading sector reforms. They can operate as individual consultants; be members of a policy institute, research organization, or consulting firm; or belong to a government agency. Each sector reform technical cooperation program must decide where to place its resources, e.g., whether to invest in strengthening the policy division in a government agency or to work energetically with a new private institute that will provide advice to key clients, such as local governments or banks. The decision is difficult, particularly at the beginning of the project when knowledge of the available resources and possibilities are limited. Whatever the arrangement, there must be a strong and continuing demand for their services. If there is not, no amount of resources will ensure success, because they will not be used.

Lesson: Defining and refining a strategy on an evolutionary basis over the first year or so of the project will probably be more effective than trying to do so during the design phase.

The decision will depend on judgments about three related factors: which investments have the greatest effect on overall reform; which investments are most likely to be sustained after donor support is withdrawn; and which organizations possess the most promising resources for the project to work with.

The decision on which investments will be most effective depends on the task to be done. If the main task ahead is further development of the legal base and production of analyses to support policy debates within government, then strengthening a federal agency could take priority, although a good institute could do much of this work *if* the government agency would or could contract for the services. But if the action has shifted significantly to the implementation phase where banks, hospitals, clinics, or particular local government agencies are the key actors, then developing the capacity of consulting firms and training organizations will be a superior investment.

To sustain reform activity when donor support has ceased, large investments in individual professionals outside an institutional context are typically a poor bet, although there are exceptions. (I give some examples later of training individual consultants as service providers.) An institute or firm active in delivering services to local governments, for example, has an obvious self-interest in building capacity so that it is not overly dependent on a single individual. Hence, those who receive advanced training are pressed to share the knowledge with others, either formally or, more likely, informally. If the person who has received the advanced training leaves the firm and the sector, others are there to carry on. Investments in the human capital of individual consultants are much more likely to be lost to the sector.

The third factor—what firms or institutes could be good partners for the firm working on sector reform—is the hardest. While there are numerous research institutes in every country of the former Soviet bloc, the great majority have turned out to be poor candidates as partners. The problems have been legion: slack management, leadership more interested in a "quick dollar" than in changing its operations, poor policy orientation, and researchers unused to working to international standards and hard deadlines. Disappointing contacts with the existing institutions have led those implementing sector reform technical cooperation projects generally to look for new firms, institutes, and individuals—including the more motivated former members of the same Soviet era institutes—with whom to work.

Often the choices are limited and sometimes they are not even really discrete. The most obvious case is when the implementing contractor elects to train a cadre of local professionals on the project staff, but after some time this cadre decides to create their own firm to continue to work in the sector. Hence, the initial decision to follow the strategy of developing a cadre of specialists without a particular institutional affiliation evolves into one in support of a new institute.

Clearly, the choice of strategy—developing individuals versus the capacity of firms or institutes, or government agencies—strongly affects the mode of capacity building. Mentoring will likely be the primary method where the contractor is committed to developing the project staff. Where there is an institutional relationship, formal training courses will be more prominent, including out-of-country training. It is possible, however, that the relationship between the contractor and a small, new firm will be particularly collegial, in which case mentoring can occur here as well. The larger and the more established the institute or firm, the less opportunity for foreign consultants to spend the necessary time mentoring institute staff.

WORKING WITH INDIVIDUALS

Nearly all sector reform projects employ local professionals. Almost all projects that use local professionals to deliver assistance to clients, such as hospitals or government agencies implementing new programs, conduct formal or informal training programs targeted on developing specific skills and conveying certain information. Few have systematic programs for staff mentoring that go beyond the formal training activities.

CASE: One part of the HSRP worked with local governments and tenant groups to create the first condominiums in about 20 cities. Because the concept of condominiums and the legislative base were new, the project had to train its own Russian staff members first, to enable them to work with the cities. A team, initially of 5 members and later of 15, was formed and taught, mostly through on-the-job training. Eventually seminars and courses were developed and taught by the team, and members new to the team could attend these courses to learn the material. A very similar process was followed by another contractor, PADCO, who worked on forming condominium associations in the eastern part of Russia.

CASE: The HSRP also provided direct assistance to about 25 banks in helping them begin lending programs for long-term loans for home purchase. A process similar to that described above was used in this case, with one significant difference. The housing finance program started much more slowly and for more than a year only two or three Russian professionals worked in this area with a U.S. consultant. This team worked with several banks. All of the Russians had very good English and received much of their on-the-job training by serving as interpreters in meetings with banks where the U.S. consultant had the lead. The Russians' development program included attending formal courses in the United States on mortgage lending and the development and presentation of mortgage courses in Russia. But a critical addition was the mentoring achieved through direct participation in numerous meetings where there was much give-and-take and discussion of complex issues and proposals—in short, covering material not found in textbooks or standard courses. The same approach was used with a single Russian professional by the Commercial Real Estate Mortgage project in Russia carried out by the Barents Group in 1995–1996.

In the HSRP, the "twinning" of short-term consultants with a Russian professional was standard practice. While this kind of in-service training is essential, it can be enriched in various ways.

CASE: The in-service training of the condominium team was supplemented with a study tour to the United States quite early in the project. The timing was important. Team members already understood the concepts and had some practical experience in Russia. Thus, they had a good basis for understanding the live examples to which they were exposed during the study tour. Officials from several cities with which the team was working were also included in the study tour. The tour was also important in educating them and in creating a solid working relationship between them and the team members.

As the team expanded in number and worked in more cities, regularly scheduled within-team "seminars" became highly useful. Experiences in different cities were discussed and the need for alterations to model legal documents and guideline brochures identified. Drafts of new materials were reviewed at such sessions. Any foreign visitor thought to possess relevant expertise was asked to address the group.

Lesson: The standard staff education vehicles of formal training seminars can be substantially enriched by conscious programs of mentoring and within-team seminars. The result will be a greater level of sophistication and understanding and consequently a group more efficient in advising program clients and thinking about further program development.

An alternative model for creating a cadre of trainers and experienced advisors to client groups is for a project to train part-time or full-time consultants to a project along with the staff. These consultants are then used by the project to deliver services for a time. Thereafter, they are free to seek market opportunities for delivering the same services. If evidence suggests that the demand for services is high even at the outset, the initial period of project support for the consultants may be dispensed with. The active use of consultants was an important element in the USAID-supported Health Reform Project in Russia and was also used effectively in a USAID-sponsored project in Poland geared to institutionalizing business training skills.

I suspect that mentoring may be much easier when the context is advising external clients—local government administrators, hospital administrators, bankers—than when the mentoring goes on in an office where the advisor attempts to upgrade the quality of products, typically reports and planning documents, produced by those with whom he is working. The wider range of dynamics in the former setting and the multiplicity of different people with whom the staff work appear to make the process both easier and more productive.[3]

WORKING WITH INSTITUTIONS

The experience of sector reform technical cooperation projects operating for three or four years is rich in working with—and even motivating creation of—local firms and policy institutes. An implementing contractor is motivated to work with local firms and institutes because it is efficient for her to do so in achieving her project's objectives. But interviews with dozens of project managers reveal that institutionalization is secondary, and is rarely thought of as a distinct goal.

The shorter the time frame for a project, the less attention given to institutionalization, understandably. But even among projects with expected lives of two or three years, strengthening firms or institutes is seldom explicit in the project. In part this lack of attention to working with and strengthening local firms results from neglecting the issue in contracts directing the work of implementing firms. There are signs of this changing, however. For example, in several contracts signed by USAID in 1995 for work in Russia, the goal of institutionalization was clearly stated, as was the encouragement of substituting local professionals for U.S. consultants. (USAID itself was motivated by calls for winding up the Russia program in a few years.) Whether this goal is realistic in projects of several months' duration remains to be seen. Also open to question is whether contractors who have ignored the institutionalization objective in the past will, in fact, respond to such requirements now.

This section discusses ways in which some contractors implementing sector reform projects have, indeed, worked at institution building. Although the many diverse experiences make a neat classification difficult, for my purposes it is useful to distinguish among the following experiences:

- contracting with local firms for discrete tasks;
- contracting with a local firm in a general partnership arrangement for implementation of the project;
- motivating creation of a new firm that takes a major, continuing role for the balance of the project; such entities can be thought of as new public policy institutes or consulting firms;
- motivating creation of a new firm that executes some discrete task for the project, typically in more of a technical support role.

In all instances we focus on local firms participating in the substantive work of the project. We exclude those simply providing logistical support.

The dynamics of the local consulting and research industry are especially important in this discussion. As new firms come online and the standards of some old-regime institutes are upgraded, the landscape can change dramatically. Importantly, the consulting industries in various countries have developed at different speeds, which precludes any general statement about the current situation in the region as a whole.

Contracting for discrete tasks. Some implementing contractors have found it effective to contract with local institutes and firms for survey work and for certain analytic studies.

CASE: The Natural Monopolies Program in Russia hired researchers primarily from the Energy Research Institute of the National Academy of Sciences to perform analyses. The Urban Institute in the HSRP contracted with several Russian teams—mostly private firms but also a National Academy of Sciences Institute—to do household survey work and for analytic studies (e.g., production of housing indicators for the country).

CASE: Research Triangle Institute as part of its Municipal Finance and Management Project in Russia hired a local management consulting firm to produce six municipal finance case studies.

The typical early experience was that a good deal of mentoring was necessary at the beginning to obtain high quality products. Careful review of analysis plans and detailed review and discussion of initial and subsequent draft products was essential to orienting the contractors to what was demanded. Little real quality control was initially provided by the institutes themselves. Quality did improve over time. While the improved skills of individuals resulting from this process are clear, it is much less clear whether the general behavior of the institutions was being modified.

Many contractors who need the services of local economists, planners, and others trained in the social sciences are not so patient. They turn away from dealing with old-style institutions to contracting with individual consultants who prove themselves capable or with the kind of new firms that I discuss below.

It is worth noting that even the early experience was more positive in contracting for more highly technical services—such as the production of computer software and engineering services. For example, in Russia for the military housing construction program a U.S. contractor, PADCO, had a positive experience in contracting with local design institutes to check proposed housing project designs.

Contracting with a partner institute. Under this arrangement, an international firm contracts with an existing host country firm or institute for a substantial array of professional services for the execution of the project. This arrangement, while once rare, is becoming more common as new capable firms are created. An early example from Russia (described in chapter 5), is of the Russian Privatization Center (RPC) working with a U.S. firm to implement a real estate information project. The RPC was involved similarly in a number of projects. Importantly, the RPC was a new institution with dynamic leadership and very close ties to the donor community via government contacts.

In general, however, foreign contractors' poor early experience with the badly motivated and misoriented old-line institutes discouraged them from creating partnerships for program implementation. Of course, many proposals to donor agencies proffered such partnerships, but few materialized during actual project execution.

Creation of new public policy institutes or consulting firms. A somewhat common pattern has been for talented former members of the elite, government-supported institutes to create their own firms in response to the opportunities afforded by the transition. Typically, they began providing consulting services to donor projects and decided that their institutes were a poor platform for such work. These new entrepreneurs were nearly universally young when they struck out on their own—few over age forty—Western-oriented, English speaking, and better-trained in Western methodology than others. Examples of the creation of such new consulting and public policy firms are legion. I focus on examples where the new firms concentrate on one or two specific sectors, and their creation and development have been closely linked to particular donor sector reform projects. I exclude new, all-purpose think tanks and those specializing in macroeconomics, as well as consulting firms with universal interests. The Urban Institute has worked with sector-specific institutes in three countries.

CASE: In 1990 two local professionals, formerly at the Institute of Sociology of the Hungarian National Academy of Sciences, founded the Metropolitan Research Institute (MRI) in Budapest to be a public policy institute on issues of housing reform and metropolitan development, including local government finances. While MRI has worked with many clients, the most important has been the USAID housing sector and municipal finance reform program. Since its creation, MRI has been a subcontractor to the Urban Institute, USAID's prime contractor for this work. Throughout the reform process, the two institutes have been real partners in carrying out a range of projects, ranging from legal reform work to designing and implementing pilot projects. In Budapest the two institutes share offices. Moreover, the Urban Institute has worked with MRI on its financial structure, and other areas, including the rules and ethos of working with international donors, to help ensure its future.

CASE: A similar story can be told of the creation of MTK Konsult in Sofia by a local professional who left her research institute in 1991 to create this new firm. Again, the foreign partner is the Urban Institute. MTK, while initially oriented to housing questions, has branched out further than MRI to work on general issues of public administration and local economic development.

Both MRI and MTK Konsult have enjoyed steady if modest growth, with full-time staff numbering about 10, and they appear to be capable of continuing to work when USAID funding is withdrawn.

CASE: The founding of the nonprofit Institute for Urban Economics (IUE) in Moscow in 1995 again features the Urban Institute. The six Russian founders of this public policy institute had all been on the staff of the Urban Institute in Moscow for several years and decided to form the new entity to continue policy development and implementation work in housing, housing finance, municipal finance, and governance issues. In this case the support of the Urban Institute was particularly strong, with UI helping set up IUE's financial structure and advising on governance issues, such as the composition and role of the Board of Trustees. USAID/Russia was also a strong supporter of this form of institutionalization.[4]

The active support of institutional development by the Urban Institute was not accidental. The team working in Eastern Europe understood very early in the process the value of strong and reliable local partners and knew it to be in its own self interest to promote creation of these firms. But they also gave a high priority to developing local capacity. The same philosophy carried over into the program in Russia but took longer to realize.[5]

CASE: The staff employed by the Harvard Institute for International Development in Russia exhibited a similar philosophy in fostering creation of both the Russian Privatization Center (RPC) and, later, the International Institute for Law-Based Economy. The latter was formed to continue work on legal reform, capital market development, and real estate reform in Russia, while RPC was formed to help execute the government's mass privatization program and then evolved into a more general consulting operation.

Inevitably the question arises as to whether the donors should be subsidizing and otherwise pushing the creation of new public policy institutes dedicated to working in one or a few sectors. The response is that force-feeding will not work. Despite the examples cited above, there are many cases of new sector-specialist firms being established by dedicated individuals that must struggle for survival. Some ultimately fail. Others never become more than a way for an individual consultant to charge overhead rather than only a consulting fee.[6] These are risky undertakings that require genuine dedication and desire to succeed. Long hours, short pay, and enormous uncertainty are often the primary characteristics of such entities. In short, while it may be possible for a donor or its contractor to create an institution with generous support in its early days, its survival will depend on the same qualities needed to sustain other start-up firms.

Lesson: The donor community and their contractors should be alert to the opportunities to foster creation of new public policy institutes with a specific sector orientation, but support them only if one is convinced that the principals of the new institute or firm have the talent, determination, and connections to make survival likely.

The rewards of successful creation can be great, worth all the difficulties. New institutions clearly dedicated to being a continuing resource for the reform and development of a particular sector bring the greatest resources to support reform when the formal donor-supported sector reform project ends. Such new firms have a base of experience that can be activated in future projects to get the most out of the available resources. A firm's experience can be especially effective when a donor wants to define a new project—either a bilateral technical assistance project or an investment project funded by a mutlilateral donor. Obviously, an experienced team will be more efficient in project implementation than an effort that has to hire and train new people. Similarly these firms can be a resource for national and local governments. However, it is questionable whether these new policy firms could survive solely on contracts from this set of clients.

Lesson: These new public policy firms are an extremely valuable resource, and the donor community should consciously seek them out as partners in future projects.

While such firms should be easily located by a contractor hired by the donors, experience suggests a tendency for foreign companies not to spend much energy identifying local resources. The donors must take the role of ensuring existing resources are utilized. Better, they should seriously consider contracting directly with the strong local firms.

Creating task-specific firms. Because of the critical role played by public policy institutes and firms, they are the focus of most discussions about creation of new entities to support sector reform. Less prominent but also important is establishment of firms to handle comparatively narrow tasks that are essential to implementation of reform.

CASE: In the Municipal Management and Finance Project in Russia, American Management Systems, a software subcontractor to Research Triangle Institute, encouraged creation of a private computer software firm in Nizhni Novgorod, which helped write the code for the financial management system being implemented there and handled installation of the computer equipment. The firm will be responsible for system maintenance when the project concludes and is positioned to offer similar services to other governments.

CASE: Similarly, the health sector reform project in Russia worked with local programmers to develop and install their information and financial management system. By spring 1996 some of them had spun off into quasi-independent firms and the project director believes some will succeed in becoming free-standing firms.

CASE: A very different example comes from the staff of the U.S. contractor PADCO, who had been working on housing sector reform in the Siberian region, with most of the team located in Novosibirsk. The staff decided to form a nonprofit entity to work with tenant groups to form and register condominiums and in other ways to support resident interests in the housing sphere throughout the region. The Public Center for Support of Housing Reform, formed with PADCO and USAID encouragement, plans to continue as a private nonprofit consulting operation after the PADCO contract ends in the fall of 1996. A key element in its business plan has been to structure itself as a membership organization, with both individuals and legal entities eligible to join. The Center hopes to attract a base of membership fee income from condominium and cooperative association members by representing the views of such associations to local governments and providing training courses and useful publications.

Often these firms stand ready to provide their services to diverse clients. The uniting element is the technical service performed. Such firms are providing critical "infrastructure services" that would be expensive for a public policy institute to provide on an in-house basis. The Public Center for Support of Housing Reform, for example, will provide expertise to various actors in the housing sector, including developers wishing to register condominium associations and local governments embarking on reforming the maintenance services in its housing stock.

Fostering creation of firms to execute these functions is typically less of a conscious objective for donors and contractors implementing sector reform projects than is the nurturing of public policy firms. And this appears appropriate given the more sophisticated tasks to be addressed by the public policy firms.

Working with government agencies. In regions outside the former Soviet bloc, the typical technical cooperation project emphasizes strengthening the capacity of government agencies responsible for carrying out a particular project. Donor-supported teams conduct detailed institutional assessments covering both the organization and its human resources. Project implementation generally includes agency reorganization and training for staff in administrative skills, economics, and accounting. In contrast, in countries of Eastern Europe and the Newly Independent States, work to improve the effectiveness of government agencies has been deemphasized. This is not surprising given that many donors perceive the role of government in the region—especially central government—as excessive. Donors see a clear need to build up the competence of lower levels of governments, private sector firms, and nongovernmental organizations as a counterbalance to central government power. Some of this work has fallen under "democratic initiative" programs; but this policy position influences sector reform work as well.

There is another reason, however, for the now-traditional institutional assessment–institutional development paradigm[7] not being applied in the region. Governments and their staffs were comparatively competent—often badly motivated, but certainly adequately educated and often possessing the necessary skills for their jobs. The real deficits have been in financial management and policy analysis, although with no real tradition of the rigorous, quantitative assessment of alternatives and benefit-cost analysis.[8] Lack of computers, copiers, and other equipment was also pervasive.

Those wishing to strengthen governments have generally had to work with the existing government structure and the inherited bureaucrats. This has also been true in the former Soviet bloc but, unlike other areas of the world, there have been important exceptions. This is because countries in the region typically created new national level ministries and often lower level offices to deal with the privatization of industry and retail and wholesale outlets. At the local level, there have also been new agencies. In Russia when the housing allowance program was implemented, every local government in the country set up small new agencies from scratch to administer it. Donors have proven more interested in working with the new agencies than with the standard line agencies, both because of their missions and because they are often headed by energetic, dedicated reformers. But even in these cases, the assistance has been on getting the job done rather than the skill enhancement or broad education so typical of institutional development projects in other regions.[9]

> CASE: The HSRP was instrumental in creation of the rent reform program under which (1) rents were being raised in Russia to cover full operating costs over a five-year period and (2) the poor were protected through implementation of the housing allowance program from paying an excessive share of their incomes for housing. The new housing allowance program needed national guidelines, which the HSRP took the lead in developing. The team also worked directly with the programs in a dozen cities, including Moscow. Training for program managers, intake workers, and others was concentrated strictly on program tasks, including operation of program software. There was no need for general skills enhancement. The usual pattern was for the team to deliver a one-day workshop on the program and provide additional advice before the city implemented the program, and then to return to deal with questions and problems as they arose. Importantly, after the initial training, city staffs quickly developed their own training programs for the new employees who were added as the program expanded. Indicative of administrators' attitudes, several cities engaged software firms to write computer programs for basic program administration functions, such as computing subsidy amounts and issuing the new payment books tenants use when paying their rent at local banks. Computerization is now common, with several software firms competing for market share.

> CASE: Similarly, the objective of the Municipal Finance and Management Project was to work in detail with local governments in several countries to set up new management and budgeting systems.

Technical training in new systems was essential but education to make up for deficiencies in basic skills was not needed.[10]

There are, of course, numerous examples of expatriate advisors being placed in ministries to enhance their effectiveness. Usually the terms of reference for these positions include mentoring local staff. But it is often difficult for the advisor to establish a good working relationship with ministry counterparts. Developing collegial relations is frequently hampered by the advisor being placed high in the hierarchy, for example as the advisor to the minister. The theory is that such placement gives the advisor the necessary access to the senior official. In fact, it makes mentoring relationships with lower level staff more difficult. This problem can be alleviated by pairing the advisor with a skilled ministry professional with whom staff feel comfortable. However, this arrangement itself can produce another problem—envy by other ministry staff of the local advisor's "special" status.

Much more infrequent has been active donor involvement in reorganizing ministries or other national level agencies or helping them add a new organization to discharge an added function.[11]

CASE: At the request of the Russian government, USAID funded the establishment of the Policy Analysis Unit in the Working Center for Economic Reform, a new agency created in the fall of 1991. The Unit works on regulatory issues surrounding natural monopolies, such as utility companies and energy transmission. The Unit is staffed by two U.S. consultants, two senior Russians, and some mid-level Russians. It prepares background analyses in support of new legislation and loan packages being readied by multilateral donors. This activity *was funded* by USAID through a contract with the IRIS Center.[12]

Indeed, it is fair to say that, compared with other regions, donors have sponsored little general institutional development for national level ministries and agencies. Rather, donor involvement with the sector reform projects is more targeted. Government staff and elected officials do participate in study tours to Western countries, some organized explicitly for them. And government officials often attend seminars organized by contractors working on sector reform where the topics are development or implementation of certain aspects of the reforms. Staff have also been exposed to stronger, quantitative analyses in the policy development process and sometimes to solid program evaluation; and in cases they have emulated these practices.

The standard forms of strengthening local governments are project-related, i.e., working with local officials to draft the necessary local normative documents and assisting them in setting up the administrative apparatus to discharge a new function. Again, study tours and seminars play a role, but much of this is one-on-one work. Importantly, local officials typically work hard at making their own contribution (producing a draft of the needed law, often with a model to work from; or proposing a new administrative structure). Advisors have generally found that local officials want to master the material and control the situation, and use advisors *as* advisors and not surrogate senior administrators.

STRENGTHENING ASSOCIATIONS

Trade and professional associations can be important vehicles for disseminating new ideas and improving technical practices. Associations have been particularly attractive clients for the donor community in the former Soviet bloc for two reasons. First, they are motivated to be active in spreading new ideas and modern practices. They must prove their worth to their members if they wish to survive. Second, strengthening associations is part of the broad program of building democratic institutions as counterweights to central government.

Associations around the world generally have two broad goals: increasing the professionalism of their members, both technical education and skills and professional ethics; and representing the interests of their members to local and national governments. Associations seek to fulfill the professionalism objective through three types of services to members: holding chapter meetings and conventions, issuing publications, and conducting training programs. The continuing nature of the contact between associations and their members and their educational role makes the pay-off from orienting the association toward market-oriented ideas and practices potentially very high.

The donor community has firmly grasped this lesson, and there are many projects aimed at creating and strengthening trade and professional associations. Some are stand-alone projects.

CASE: In the early days of the transition, USAID entered into a cooperative agreement with the Eastern European Real Property

Foundation, a subsidiary of the National Association of Realtors in the United States. The objective of the foundation is exactly the creation and strengthening of real estate trade associations—associations of realtors, property appraisers, and property managers. By 1993 the foundation was working in several Eastern European countries and in the Ukraine and the Russian Federation.

But more common is for sector reform projects to work in the same direction as the relevant associations.

CASE: Within the USAID-supported health sector reform project in the Russian Federation, the contractor, Abt Associates, identified several associations as useful transmitters of information about new practices. The project gave grants of $50,000 to $75,000 to three associations. Grants for issuing publications to members went to the Association of Don [River Basin] Physicians and to the Moscow Association of Health Insurance Organizations, while the All-Russia Nurses Association received a grant for general development.

CASE: The HSRP entered into an agreement with the Russian association of Mortgage Banks under which it provided the association with a full-time trainer, training materials, and computer and photocopying equipment. The Program also team taught numerous courses with association trainers.

CASE: USAID supported the Private Construction Contractors Association of Slovakia. In this case, start-up grants to the association covered the salary of the executive director along with certain other direct costs, accounting for about 40 percent of the association's budget.

CASE: The Local Government Initiative (LGI) Project in Bulgaria has worked with three regional associations of cities and was instrumental in establishing the Foundation for Local Government Reform, a small national-level advocacy and policy development institution. The LGI has employed a resident advisor to work intensively with these entities on organizational and governance issues. The associations have cooperated with the Foundation to provide training to their member cities, including training for newly elected mayors and to officials on activities to promote economic development.

It is logical for assistance to associations as part of sector reform projects to be more effective than independent projects to strengthen them. One reason is the greater knowledge of the issues facing association members possessed by sector specialists compared with "association builders." Another is that the sector reform program provides more relevant materials for publications and courses. The reform project and the association could jointly lobby the government and legislature for needed legal and regulatory changes.

Beyond providing funds and technical materials, which can serve as the basis for association publications, donor projects frequently provide training to association leadership on such topics as recruiting members, understanding the types of membership services to provide, and financial management. A substantial part of such courses are offered in the donor's home country. For example, USAID/Russia sponsored courses in the United States during 1996 on association development.

Associations have typically been responsive to the goals of the assistance provided, but not always.

CASE: The Russian Association of Mortgage Banks, which was assisted by the HSRP as described above, rejected some of the mortgage finance courses developed by the project on the ground that they were too "theoretical." The association's leadership reported that those attending some of the courses found the short-term pay-off of working through a general curriculum on a particular topic, such as management of financial risks, to be less interesting than listening to a dozen presentations on various subjects by practicing bankers. In any event, the association added the latter type of seminars to its offerings, partially at the expense of teaching the more structured courses. The project turned to other associations and teaching institutes to continue to offer the more structured banking courses.

This example may illustrate a healthy development: the association rejecting outside advice or assistance in favor of responding to its members—and thereby surviving.

To my knowledge there has been no systematic examination of the pay-off to activities assisting in the creation or in the strengthening of trade and professional associations. My sense is that the expenditures involved have generally been modest, and so the benefits can likewise be modest and the investment still deemed reasonable. The test of the effectiveness of will come when outside assistance is with-drawn.

Lesson: Trade and professional associations can play an important role in furthering sector reform. But managers of sector reform technical cooperation projects must be prepared to be flexible in working with trade and professional associations. Be ready for differences in short-term objectives to materialize, and deal with them in a way not destructive of the basic relationship.

Notes

1. Strengthening government agencies is the closest link between institutionalization as discussed here and the traditional institutional development activities implemented by donors in other regions. One example is creation of a policy division in the relevant ministry. For a description of traditional development activities see, for example, Brinkerhoff (1994). In the former Soviet Union the range of clients appears to be wider than in other regions.

2. In the Housing Sector Reform Program the Urban Institute strategy was to reserve use of study tours to the United States for developmental activities, i.e., to help Russians with whom a team is working on the initial design and implementation of an innovation understand how the innovation works in practice. Examples include a visit by Moscow officials involved in the first competition for selecting a private firm to replace state firms and a visit by several lawyers and State Duma members to see certain aspects of the mortgage lending process as a basis for drafting the Law on Mortgage.

3. For discussion of the difficulties encountered in standard mentoring/training in institutional development projects see World Bank (1982) and Muscat (1986: 84–5).

4. The Urban Institute was also instrumental in creating an urban-oriented consulting firm in Prague.

5. U.S. foundations have been active in supporting new nonprofit public policy institutes in Eastern Europe. Some joined forces to provide grant funds to the Hudson Institute to work with these institutions to upgrade their fund raising and management practices. Most of the institutes assisted deal with macroeconomic issues; sector specialist institutes are less common generally and are more often created as for-profit entities, which places them outside the group that can be helped by U.S. foundations. See Quigley (1995) for an overview of U.S. foundations' activities in the region.

6. Anyone working on a sector reform project for several years will have a list of firms that fit the descriptions just given. In Russia, in the housing and urban sector, surviving private firms include the H-Center, the Leontief Center, Polis-3, and the Agency for Urban Research and Consulting.

7. See, for example, Brinkerhoff (1994), Muscat (1986), World Bank (1993).

8. Rather, training at the elite research institutes was directed to optimization modeling. For the case of the Soviet Union, see Sutela (1991).

9. It is worth noting that the traditional institutional development projects have led generally to disappointing results and the broad trend has been to tie such projects more closely to sector reform projects (Muscat 1986: 82–4).

10. This project is briefly described in Annex B.

11. Schiavo-Campo (1994) suggests the creation of "efficient nuclei" within existing ministries to promote institutional change.

12. This project is further described in Annex B.

Chapter Eight

WHAT'S TO BE DONE?

A successful technical cooperation program in support of sector reform is a hard-won achievement. The project must be well designed, implemented creatively and flexibly, and have the active support of host country counterparts—from senior government officials to bankers, to hospital, farm, or other administrators, to city officials. A sector reform program must be multifarious, and structuring it is clearly an intellectually demanding task. Leaders of design and implementation teams must be good managers and have significant technical knowledge of the sector, deep experience operating in complicated policy environments, and, ideally, some years of working outside their home country. Additionally, they must have a "vision" of sector reform—an almost intuitive understanding of how reform should unfold and how each achievement in the sector can be best exploited. In short, they must always be one step ahead of developments. All this requires a great deal of self-confidence. But it requires more than that. It requires, at the same time, an ability to operate quietly behind the scenes and to work hard planning for the project's own obsolescence—by strengthening local analysts, administrators, and institutions to replace the project at its conclusion.

Not many project managers—either at donor agencies or the consultants who execute most projects—possess this full array of skills. Moreover, the design of projects often militates against success. I seek, in this book, to make project success less dependent upon an outstanding performance by the project manager. I do so by offering a series of prescriptions for managers on how to increase the odds of project success by cataloguing lessons acquired through direct field experience. These lessons can go a long way to reducing a project's reliance on any single "exceptional" person. I begin this chapter by collecting them all together for easy reference.

My second section draws a set of conclusions that I hope will be helpful to managers at donor institutions, whether they be bilateral organizations, such as USAID or the British Know How Fund, or multilateral giants such as the World Bank or the European Union. I then offer the actual project managers specific advice. In both cases I repeat the most salient points from the prior discussion and, in cases, amplify them as well.

I end the chapter and the book by looking ahead at how general developments in the region may affect the likelihood of success of sector reform projects. I also give one vision of how the ingredients of a successful project may differ in the future compared with those of an early transition period.

SUMMARY OF LESSONS LEARNED

Defining the Project

Use a "menu" approach to guide the discussion between the donor and local officials. This should be an annotated list of areas on which the project is prepared to work, which should be translated for distribution to meeting participants.

Involve local technical experts as early as possible in the design process.

Project designs that force-feed resources into the project start-up through overly ambitious time schedules are a mistake. Projects should start small and expand as additional resources can be effectively employed.

Donor managers should reexamine the underlying premises of the project immediately after contract award, before recruiting long-term advisors and otherwise launching the project. An additional fact-finding mission at the start of the contract is not what is needed. If the donor has established good local contacts—officials or consultants—during the definition stage, those contacts can quickly inform the donor of significant changes affecting the project, to allow immediate modification of the statement of work.

Donors should work hard at discovering what their counterparts are already doing in a sector before launching a new activity. I acknowledge the difficulty of doing this well for all the possible bilateral programs. Hence, project definition teams sent to the field must be given the work of identifying other projects as an explicit task in their terms of reference. A strong effort must be made thereafter to ensure coordination on an ongoing basis.

Donors must be clear about their expectations regarding the contractor's relations with local professionals in the project. Where mentoring and staff development are an objective and where local professionals are expected to have real responsibility, it must be clearly stated in the contract. This step is critical to capacity building and institutionalization.

Donors should rethink their prohibitions against those working on project design being barred from project implementation. At a minimum more of the knowledge gained by consultants doing the design work must be transferred to the implementation team.

Achieving Credibility

Project start-up is facilitated by defining a few initial tasks with some precision and for these tasks to be clearly agreed upon by all relevant parties prior to the arrival of the implementation team. Importantly, if the initial tasks are clearly defined, this information can be used in recruiting advisors. Having the right people present to work on the initial tasks obviously accelerates the work.

Define the initial tasks to demonstrate real progress early in the project. Other activity can and should be going on at the same time, but concentrate on achieving a demonstrable, even if limited, success.

To enhance its credibility the technical cooperation team should seek opportunities to assist its clients with critical tasks. Often this will require the team extending itself—working over the weekend or having to push hard to meet urgent client requests and continue progress on its demonstration program. An important result of helping in a pinch is that word spreads that the team is serious about its work. This has the snowballing effect of helping other aspects of the technical cooperation program go more easily.

Tailor advice and recommendations for the local context, even if it requires a good deal of extra work. Going out of one's way to make the advice immediately applicable helps win rapport with the client by convincing him that the consulting team understands the local situation and that the team genuinely wants to provide usable assistance.

Delivering the Services

Comprehensive sector reform technical cooperation projects require a resident advisor to coordinate all activities in the project and to make needed ongoing adjustments to the work program. But host country clients should be given real responsibility for making changes. Use of expatriate advisors should be limited to those tasks that local staff, consultants, or firms cannot do. Since there will be numerous tasks for which short-term advice is appropriate, however, projects should not adopt a "residents only" policy. It is both expensive and inefficient.

Heavy involvement of local professionals in sector technical cooperation projects will increase project efficiency and productivity and should be an integral part of all but the smallest, most limited projects.

Few contractors will naturally give a major role in the implementation of sector reform projects to local professionals. Therefore, donor contracts should contain provisions requiring it, and donor oversight of implementation should include this area. A promising idea, already embodied in some contracts, is to require that the share of professional services to be delivered by local professionals increase over the life of the project.

Monitoring and evaluation are important elements in a sector technical cooperation program because they provide the basis for rapid policy interventions and midcourse corrections in projects. They deserve more attention from the donors and implementers alike.

The fewer separate contracts or separate projects in a sector reform technical cooperation program, the easier will be intraprogram coordination and the greater the efficiency of the overall program. The need to show results quickly can be addressed by proper program phasing, as indicated in an earlier lesson about concentrating early in a project on a few tasks, and through a strong monitoring component, which will generate hard information on project accomplishments.

Donors should avoid organizing projects as a sequential set of short-term contracts (six to nine months) in order to maximize control over the project. They run the grave risk of substantial turnover in resident foreign consultants and enormous resource costs as a result. Contractors should have as a constant goal to minimize the number of short-term advisors on a project. Where new advisors must be introduced, before meeting with local counterparts, they should be made thoroughly knowledgeable, not only about the project but also about conditions in the country.

Beyond Demonstrations

In considering whether a pilot project can be replicated on a significant scale, check to be certain that the incentives to key actors—local officials and/or service providers—to carry out the reform are in fact positive and perceived clearly.

Do not force-feed assistance in the roll-out phase. Offer assistance to a large group of clients and work more or less intensively with each in accordance with the interest each exhibits.

Station people full time at a client's location—be it a bank, an enterprise, or a municipal government—only after fully satisfying oneself that alternative arrangements will not be adequate to provide intensive-enough assistance. The risk of underutilized resources is too great. Centrally based mobile teams will often be the superior option for delivering advice.

Institutionalizing Reform

Instructor's guides and in-depth training for trainers on a particular subject are warranted only for courses for which there will likely be a lasting demand.

Identify appropriate institutions, including trade associations and training institutes, with whom to jointly offer courses and seminars.

Substitute local for foreign instructors quickly, even if it means extra expatriate training of trainers in the first offerings.

Do not oversupply the market.

Defining and refining a strategy on an evolutionary basis over the first year or so of the project will probably be more effective than trying to do so during the design phase.

The standard staff education vehicles of formal training seminars can be substantially enriched by conscious programs of mentoring and within-team seminars. The result will be a greater level of sophistication and understanding and consequently a group more efficient in advising program clients and thinking about further program development.

The donor community and its contractors should be alert to the opportunities to *foster* creation of new public policy institutes with a specific sector orientation, but support them only if one is convinced that the principals of the new institute or firm have the talent, determination, and connections to make survival likely.

These new public policy firms are an extremely valuable resource, and the donor community should consciously seek them out as partners in future projects.

Trade and professional associations can play an important role in furthering sector reform. But managers of sector reform technical cooperation projects must be prepared to be flexible in working with trade and professional associations. Be ready for differences in short-term objectives to materialize, and deal with them in a way not destructive of the basic relationship.

A WORD TO THE DONORS

I titled this chapter "What's to be done?" rather than using the equally famous question of the same historic moment in the Russian Revolution, "Who is guilty?" My objective is not to assess blame but to move forward. Administrators at donor agencies are under strong pressure to demonstrate that technical cooperation projects yield clear results quickly. The expectations among the legislative bodies voting the funds for these projects may have reached truly unrealistic levels, but this does nothing to relieve the pressures on administrators. Less than dramatic results from technical projects are blamed, first, on administering agencies, and second, on maladroit and avaricious contractors.

My sense is that the quest for "instant results" has led to impatience with careful and comprehensive design of sector reform programs and has strongly militated in favor of smaller, more discrete projects. These hold the promise of visible results in a short term—perhaps a few months—and a high benefit-cost ratio seems to be implied. The fact is, however, that these "program shards," however meritorious, will not add up to a sector reform program and the money spent will, ultimately, have been poorly invested if sector reform is the objective. The opportunity cost of the resources expended to achieve these irretrievably limited objectives is high indeed.

ADVICE FOR PROGRAM ADMINISTRATORS

This section lays out advice for program administrators in six areas that, in my judgment, are in dire need of constructive change.

1. *Take a comprehensive perspective on sector reform.* I argue repeatedly in this volume for the necessity of including five elements in a sector reform technical cooperation program: development of the legal structure, demonstration projects, monitoring and evaluation, dissemination of results, and institutionalization. Each of these is essential to maximizing the chance of success. If they are not all

by many donors governing the competitions for selecting a contractor to implement the project prevent exploiting the expertise developed in designing the project. Much more effort should be devoted to resolving the conundrum of maintaining reasonable competition and realizing a higher return on the investment in consultant resources made during the design phase.

5. *Observe three rules in managing project start-up.* These are for administrators in donor organizations during the time when the tender process is underway and prior to initial implementation. First, continue limited technical cooperation activity during the tender process if the time between reaching agreement with the host government about the project and initiation of fieldwork by the permanent party is likely to exceed three months. Failure to do so costs the project momentum that will never be regained. At the same time, be careful in choosing the activity for this period. Initial work on a demonstration project often is a good target, although in some cases there is a very pressing need for assistance on development of legislation.

Second, at the conclusion of the tender process and before finalizing the appointment of the chief-of-party, check to be certain that the assumptions underlying the project's design have not changed during the tender period. If there has been ongoing preproject activity in the country, this will be simple. Otherwise, checking will have to be done with host country government officials and the local professionals engaged during the project identification.

Third, pay close attention to selection of the project manager. It is hard to overstate the importance of properly recruiting for this position. The proposed manager will be a key part of the proposals reviewed, and the selection of the winning bid will be heavily influenced by the person nominated. But it is important to go beyond the paper record. As part of the competitive process, a full interview with the proposed project managers is important in obtaining information on personality as well as technical knowledge. Telephone calls to prior clients to check performance, an obvious step, is infrequently taken.

6. *Management oversight during implementation.* Beyond carefully reviewing the project's workplan and its periodic status reports, and taking remedial action where necessary to shore up weak project execution, several important tasks fall to the donor's project manager. The task for which there is no substitute for manager responsibility is coordinating with other donors on projects in the sector. While it is true that consultants working on projects in the same sector generally "run into each other" during the course of project execution, it is by then frequently too late to prevent duplication and even overt

competition for the attention of senior officials. Even where collegial relations do exist among contractors, donor coordination on project planning is essential.

The second oversight task is to ensure that proper monitoring of project activities and impacts are undertaken and reported upon in a readily usable way. Such information is clearly to the advantage of the donor's program manager, as it puts him or her in a strong position to report on the project. Brief status and budget reports will not satisfy this objective. Building periodic reports on agreed-upon indicators in the statement of work is a minimum condition for obtaining useful data.

The kind of information generated through monitoring activities can be an important element in identifying implementation problems. Indicators showing little progress are likely to mean that the program is churning rather than moving forward. Where such problems arise, the program manager must be involved in adopting solutions, although it is normally desirable to give the chief-of-party an initial opportunity to suggest a shift in approach.

Lastly, a job that has not occupied program managers enough in the past has been working with the contractors on the twin tasks of ensuring proper use of host country professionals and institutionalization of reforms. My sense is that most contractors will show little enthusiasm for these tasks unless pressured by the client to undertake them. Explicit guidance based on what works in other projects, as well as encouragement more generally, will often be necessary.

ADVICE FOR CHIEFS-OF-PARTY AND SENIOR CONSULTANTS

Those lessons from the sector reform projects to date in the former Soviet bloc that I believe contain the greatest potential for increasing the odds of successful project implementation are emphasized here. They concern the post-contract award phase of the project. I recognize that many project managers operate under real constraints embodied in project design and administrative procedures required by their contracts. Common problems include significant elements of a comprehensive reform program missing from the project, a bias against giving serious responsibility to host country professionals, and lack of flexibility given to the chief-of-party, so that he or she must constantly check with the donor's project manager for permission to proceed to the next phase, undertake small additional tasks on an opportunistic basis, or make modest midcourse corrections. These constraints notwithstanding, contractors do, in fact, have substantial, if not complete, control over the practices I focus on here, if they are consistently strong-minded and persistent about pursuing them.

1. *Employ local professionals, give them real responsibility, and treat them as full colleagues.* I rank this lesson first both because of its importance for project success and because of the frequency with which contractors ignore local professionals as a resource. Locating outstanding local professionals takes time and judgment. And once hired, they will need careful supervision in the beginning and mentoring throughout. But for all the reasons stated in chapters 3 and 4, they can have a large positive impact on project implementation. Begin with a couple of senior professionals, and expand the number in the team as the workload expands and the initial hires can do some of the mentoring of the new people.

2. *Begin project implementation quickly but initially work on a limited set of tasks to win credibility for the program.* The loss of momentum caused by the contracting process often undermines support for the project among host country officials. Project start-up problems seem to grow exponentially as the number of months grows between the project definition mission and the launch of implementation. Get to the field as soon as possible. Even if the chief-of-party must shuttle between home and the country for a few months before permanent relocation (but with the great majority of time in the field), it is worth it.

Once there, on the administrative side, have the initial round of meetings with client officials to confirm the project definition and the importance of the early tasks to be undertaken. Recruit local staff. And set up shop. During this phase, start work on one or two substantive tasks that will have visible results to the host country clients within a few months. Often these constitute the design phase of a demonstration project. Local officials know you have been busy when you bring the detailed design to them for review, along with the request for whatever formal permissions and coordination are needed to begin actual implementation. In some cases the most pressing tasks will turn out to be assisting with the drafting of new laws or implementing regulations for recently passed laws. Be prepared to respond quickly and well to urgent requests for support in this area, even if you and your principal client had agreed to focus on a demonstration project initially. Expect crises to produce opportunities for the project to prove its usefulness.

The corollary to the foregoing is that, in the early months of the project, monitoring and evaluation, dissemination, and institutionalization can all be put on the back burner. The chief-of-party should be thinking about how to organize these activities, being stimulated by what he or she observes about the resources with which to work. But get the principal elements of the project working smoothly and gain credibility before acting in the other areas.

3. *Remember that expanding a pilot program to a broader scale differs fundamentally from implementing the pilot itself.* Time and again contractors and donors treat expansion of a successful demonstration program essentially as doing more of the same, i.e., using the same blend of inputs as for the initial pilots. In fact, succeeding rounds of demonstrations require a different approach. Less expatriate expertise is needed and less time should have to be spent with each client (i.e., bank, polyclinic, firm, or local government agency). More of the knowledge transfer should happen through formal courses and seminars. Generally avoid stationing staff with a single client, because of the loss in flexibility entailed. Importantly, the "roll-out" approach should be much cheaper per client than the initial pilot.

Finally, be sure to work with clients that are ready for change. Avoid being restricted to a list of cities or banks or other clients that the donor selects for reasons having nothing to do with this particular project. Working with unmotivated clients practically guarantees low productivity for the project. Rather, offer services to a larger group of clients than is likely to move forward with reform, and focus the available resources on those who demonstrate progress.

4. *Institutionalization = training + capacity building.* Most chiefs-of-party will be inexperienced when it comes to formulating a plan for the kind of institutionalization desirable in the countries of the former Soviet bloc. Of the two channels leading to institutionalization, working with local organizations to create and sustain training programs promoting sector reform is by far the more straightforward.

With respect to building local capacity, it is impossible to give much guidance on which of the many options will be superior *a priori*. A couple of points are clear, however. First, investments in strengthening *institutions* are more likely to produce continuing benefits for the sector than investments in the human capital of individuals. Second, creating new institutions—consulting firms or nonprofit public policy institutes—is much more demanding than building up existing entities. The key is to be flexible about how to proceed and not to act too soon. Beyond staff mentoring, several months at least will typically be required to gather information on the relevant options and make an informed decision.

THE FUTURE

Looking ahead from the fall of 1996, I envision two groups of clients for sector reform projects among the countries of the former Soviet bloc. On the one hand, there will be second- and third-generation projects in the heart of Eastern Europe—in Hungary, Poland, the Czech and Slovak Republics, the Baltics, and other fast starters. On the other hand, there will be first- and second-generation projects in countries further east, including most of those of the former Soviet Union and southeastern Europe, such as Albania and Romania.

In both sets of countries the future working environment will be different from the early years of the economic and political transition. The donor community must take the evolving situation into account if the chances of success are to be raised in the next generation of projects. Here are my guesses about what lies ahead.

THE EVOLVING ENVIRONMENT

One can argue that, in the future, successful project implementation will be more difficult in both groups of countries. Pressure for change has diminished in many countries. In part, this is a natural response to the wholesale change already achieved—reform fatigue on the part of the population. In part, this results from the maturation of the political process in which those who want to protect the existing benefits organize to achieve their goals. Whatever the cause, passing the necessary legislation will generally be more difficult in the future than in the early years of transition.

Another factor at work is disillusionment in the countries themselves with the donor community and outside experts. The cumulative impact of successive waves of "donor tourists," who contribute little in only marginally successful projects, has soured many officials on technical cooperation projects. This does not mean that they will refuse to cooperate. Rather, their enthusiasm will be muted. And they are likely to want evident progress in project implementation before they invest much of their own capital.[1] In this milieu, projects embodying both capital assistance and technical cooperation will likely enjoy a comparatively greater advantage in gaining serious attention of national government officials over simple technical cooperation projects than in the past.

The outlook is not entirely pessimistic. There are reasons to believe that sector reform projects may work more efficiently in the future. First, host country counterparts—ranging from national-level officials to local administrators—have learned from working with expatriate teams what to expect and how such teams operate. This means, especially, that project definition should be more realistic and more efficient than before.

Second, local capacity for project implementation has increased enormously, thereby facilitating this part of the work. In many countries local firms have been created by the more talented, more energetic, and more dedicated researchers from the old state institutes. Even sector specialty firms or public policy institutes exist in some countries. These new entities stand ready to work with foreign consulting firms. And they are supplemented in several countries by branch offices of the big international accounting and consulting firms—another resource that can be tapped. All of this means that the tasks of recruiting local partners and institutionalization may be much easier in the years ahead, although it would be facile to suggest that new projects will rely on everything falling into place nicely.

Third, a cadre of chiefs-of-party and senior donor managers has emerged with not only practical but also positive experience in the region. This is an obvious resource to be exploited, if the ranks of the consultants are not too severely thinned by senior consultants returning to their prior careers after a stint in a country of the former Soviet bloc.

INGREDIENTS FOR SUCCESS

The fundamentals of good sector technical cooperation projects are unlikely to change, in my view. But the context is evolving rapidly and to be successful in the future, projects may well have to be introduced and structured differently from those in the past.

Gaining Acceptance. Future projects may well have greater difficulty in enlisting active cooperation from host country counterparts than in the past, for reasons sketched earlier. Several actions on the part of donor managers and their contractors could be decisive in this regard. First, it will be essential that they understand the maturing of the thinking and experience of their counterparts. Nearly all countries in the region are long past the stage at which presentations about how the market works or how certain tasks are done in the West—running hospitals, managing housing, municipal budgeting, the basics of underwriting loans—are of interest in and of themselves. The better professionals in every sector have achieved a general level of such knowledge. Many also have practical experience, as housing developers, health sector managers, real estate appraisers, and so forth. A donor that intends to launch a project in a sector new to it cannot afford to take a naive, uninformed approach in which a general offer of assistance will any longer be viewed as valuable.

Second, the donor managers and their contractors must be thoroughly conversant with previous or ongoing work sponsored by the donor agency and others *before* discussions with senior officials. Granted, the limited effective cooperation among the donors is a problem in this area. But this does not exonerate those seeking cooperation from having the relevant information.

The credibility of newcomers is on the line. And the difference in the reception recorded can be dramatic—the difference between polite interest by a midlevel official and a serious discussion at the deputy minister level of a concrete project. To be sure, offers of assistance will rarely be refused. But they can be shunted to a fairly unproductive use. I know of cooperation projects with Russian ministries in which new donors are essentially assigned a couple of cities or a region in which to work on certain sectoral topics with which the ministry has already had substantial experience. The work may be beneficial to the regions but the ministries do not expect any lessons of national importance to emerge. Indeed, the ministries sometimes view these as rewards to regional colleagues who will make study tours to interesting places as part of the program. As bilateral programs proliferate, more of this can be expected.

Third, active cooperation will be more likely if host country counterparts see more direct benefits from the work already done for their countrymen. There is often a palpable difference in attitude if it is clear from the outset that a large share of the work will be done by local organizations rather than by a group of foreign experts. As more local professionals become experts in various fields, ministries and other counterparts are more and more likely to make the involvement of local professionals a binding test.[2]

Evolving Activities. I see two directions in which effective technical cooperation projects may evolve in the future. The first is straightforward. As the sophistication of local professionals increases, the composition of technical cooperation projects should shift to take this into account: (a) the contribution of foreign expertise will be increasingly restricted to senior project management and ever more technically sophisticated tasks, and (b) the foreign share of the total level of effort will steadily decline.

The second direction of change concerns the scope of projects. In many sectors the first-generation, broad-gauge reforms will have been implemented. Second-generation reforms will typically be more targeted and more refined. The need for a comprehensive overall approach to sector technical cooperation projects will be even greater than in the past, if anything, but the importance of various components will change. Within the overall project the necessity of monitoring sectoral developments and conducting evaluations of the effects and impacts of early reform will be of increasing importance for identifying where resources at the margin can best be employed. Often revised legislation or regulations will be needed to overcome problems identified in the course of implementing reforms or, for businesses, refined procedures associated with offering new products or services—leasing operations and commercial real estate lending by banks, for example.

In some instances, demonstration projects will be critical to gaining acceptance of further reforms or simply determining feasibility. An interesting case illustrating the possibilities for a demonstration project to pave the way for major reform is the newly launched pilot implementation of a radically changed property tax system in two Russian cities, mounted to test its administrative complexity and revenue generation potential.

Increasing the policy development capabilities of government agencies and private public policy organizations offers other future opportunities to the donor community. The rising prominence of rigorous program monitoring and evaluation for sustaining successful reform should create a heightened interest in such work. Modern social science techniques for program evaluation were virtually absent in the region prior to the transition. So there is little to build on. While mentoring as part of donor-supported projects including evaluation is one track, it is by definition limited. Development of short courses on policy analysis and evaluation for midcareer national officials will be a key ingredient. But an even broader approach is needed. One possibility is to integrate such courses into the generally highly developed continuing education systems in the region, through a comprehensive program of textbook development and training of trainers.

The design and implementation of sector reform technical assistance projects is likely to remain a highly demanding undertaking with the odds of success no better than even. The donor community would prefer better odds. But the pay-off of success, when achieved, should not be underestimated. Improving the efficiency of a major sector in a country's economy can easily be the equivalent of generating an additional percentage point of Gross Domestic Product. Donor expenditures on the reform projects are, by comparison, tiny. Thus, even the *average* rate of return to the donors' investment is very high indeed if projects succeed. My thesis is that the odds can be improved further by exploiting lessons like those that I and others have learned through implementation of "first wave" projects in the region.

Notes

1. This point was made in mid-1996 by the team implementing the Local Government Initiative in Bulgaria. In the project's revised work plan, they make the point that mayors had developed a more sophisticated approach to donor assistance. They then stated, "Simply put, the new group of mayors expects a greater level of results and impacts from donor assistance and is less fascinated than their predecessors with the presence of an American advisor" (Hoffman et al. 1996: 5).

2. At the same time, donors and project managers should identify their own local partners, i.e., they should not rely on suggestions from ministry or other officials, which too often turn out to be referrals to old colleagues who are incapable of actually doing the assignments.

THE HOUSING SECTOR REFORM PROGRAM IN THE RUSSIAN FEDERATION

by Nadezhda B. Kosareva

BRIEF HISTORY AND MAIN PHASES OF PROGRAM

Project Planning

The design of the USAID (U.S. Agency for International Development)/ Urban Institute Shelter Cooperation Program (also known as the Housing Sector Reform Program [HSRP]) and its initial implementation were executed by The Urban Institute under contract to USAID, as part of the Institute's ongoing work on housing and city planning problems in various countries. This contract enabled work to begin several months prior to the USAID's signing a contract with The Urban Institute to implement the Housing Sector Reform I Program in the Russian Federation and in Moscow, which was concluded on September 1, 1992. (See table A.1 for a full chronology of the contracting of the project, agreements signed with different governing bodies, and the main focus of work under each phase.)

Raymond Struyk, then director of the International Activities Center at The Urban Institute and the future program director of the Housing Sector Reform Program, visited Moscow on an information-gathering trip in November 1991. At that time, he met with Nadezhda B. Kosareva, a Russian specialist in housing sector reform who had been recommended to the program as a prospective consultant to facilitate initial activities in Russia. (Kosareva, a senior research scientist at the Institute for Economic Forecasting of the Russian Academy of Sciences, is an expert in housing construction forecasts, housing demand simulations, and regional housing programs. From the start of the program, Kosareva served as a consultant, becoming deputy program director after 18 months and later head of the Russian Fund "The Institute for Urban Economics," an independent nonprofit organization formed in 1995 by the Russian consultants to the program.

Table A.1 CHRONOLOGY OF URBAN INSTITUTE WORK ON HOUSING SECTOR REFORM PROGRAM UNDER USAID CONTRACTS—USAID/RUSSIAN FEDERATION AND USAID/REGIONAL ADMINISTRATION AGREEMENTS: NOVEMBER 1991–MARCH 1996

Stages of program identification and implementation	USAID/UI contracts	Agreements between USAID and the Russian Federation	Agreements between USAID and regional and municipal governments
HSRP I identification, design, and initial implementation: November 1991–September 1992	"Housing and Urban Programs Worldwide Technical Support Programs." Signed: 9/28/90. Period of Performance: 9/28/90–9/27/96.		
HSRP I implementation: September 1992–present	"Housing Sector Reform Project." Signed: 9/01/92. Period of Performance: 9/01/92–8/31/97. Main Tasks: Housing legal reform and selected demonstration projects in Russian Federation and City of Moscow.	"Memorandum of Understanding between Russian Federation and the U.S. Agency for International Development." Signed: 3/25/92. Agreed by: A. Nechayev, Minister of Economy of Russia; B. Furmanov, Minister of Architecture, Construction, Housing Facilities and Community Services of Russia; S. Vasilyev, Director of the Economic Reforms Working Center under the Government of the Russian Federation; David Olinger, Assistant Director, Office of Housing and Urban Programs, USAID. Period of Performance: 2 years.	"Memorandum of Understanding between USAID and the City of Moscow for Technical Assistance in the Housing Sector." Signed: 3/23/92. Agreed by: Y. Luzhkov, Premier of the Moscow City Government; D. Olinger, Assistant Director, Office of Housing and Urban Programs, USAID. Confirmed by: A. Matrosov, Chairman of Mosinzhkomitet and Moscow Government Minister; A. Bryachikhin, Prefect, Moscow Government Minister; P. Saprykin, Chairman of Moszhilkomitet and Moscow Government Minister.

Main Tasks:

Legal Framework for Housing: In the short term, the primary focus will be clarification and development of needed regulatory laws for the Housing Law, the City Planning Law, and the corresponding Housing and City Planning Codes and regulations dealing with other housing aspects—for example, housing finance. *Housing Finance:* Design of the housing finance system, including development of legislation and regulations; technical issues of the type of mortgage instruments to employ; methods of mobilizing funds for housing lending; formation of the mortgage savings banks, and creation of necessary mortgage loan underwriting, origination, and servicing procedures.

"Agreement between the Government of the United States of America and the Government of the Russian Federation for Technical Assistance in the Housing Sector"

Signed: 7/11/94.

Period of Performance: 2 years.
The initial main area of cooperation is the organization of the system of management of the City housing stock and ways to improve the efficiency in the maintenance of the municipal housing stock. The primary task will be to experiment with alternative management arrangements, particularly the introduction of private management companies on a competitive basis for housing maintenance.

"Memorandum of Understanding for Technical Cooperation in the Development of Mortgage Lending between Mosbusinessbank and USAID"

Signed: 11/23/92.

Agreed by:
V. Bukato, President of Mosbusinessbank;
James Norris, Director, USAID, Russian Federation.

Period of Performance: 2 years.

"Agreement between USAID and the Government of the City of Moscow for Technical Assistance in the Housing Sector"

Signed: 7/28/94.

Table A.1   CHRONOLOGY OF URBAN INSTITUTE WORK ON HOUSING SECTOR REFORM PROGRAM UNDER USAID CONTRACTS—USAID/RUSSIAN FEDERATION AND USAID/REGIONAL ADMINISTRATION AGREEMENTS: NOVEMBER 1991–MARCH 1996 (continued)

Stages of program identification and implementation	USAID/UI contracts	Agreements between USAID and the Russian Federation	Agreements between USAID and regional and municipal governments
		Agreed by: E. Basin, Minister, State Committee of Architecture and Construction of Russia; A. Vavilov, First Deputy Minister of Finance of Russia; S. Vasilyev, Deputy Minister of Economy of Russia; James Norris, Director, USAID, Russian Federation. *Period of Performance:* 2 years. *Principal Areas for Mutual Work and Assistance:* (1) Continued assistance in the development of laws necessary for structuring of the housing sector along market principles and of the corresponding implementing regulations. (2) Continued assistance in implementing the program of increasing fees and communal services and the simultaneous introduction of housing allowances for lower-income families. (3) Continued work on introduction of condominiums in the Federation. (4) Continued work with private banks to foster development of the housing finance	*Agreed by:* Y. Luzhkov, Premier of the Moscow City Government; J. Norris, Director, USAID, Russian Federation. *Period of Performance:* 2 years. *The principal areas for mutual work and assistance to the government by American and Russian experts are:* (1) Continued assistance in the introduction of private firms, competitively selected, for the maintenance of municipal housing. (2) Continued assistance in implementing the program of increasing fees for maintenance and communal services and the simultaneous introduction of housing allowances for lower-income families. (3) Continued work with the City Administration on the introduction of condominiums in the City. (4) Continued work with the City Administration and the private banks to foster the development of the housing finance system in the City and to begin long-term mortgage lending on market

system in the Russian Federation to begin long-term mortgage lending on market principles. Special attention will be devoted to development of the Agency for Mortgage Lending and the Association of Mortgage Banks.

(5) Additional support to regional governments to formulate and implement housing reforms.

(6) Initiate a program of advice to the Russian Federation government on land policy and experimentation with selected local governments on market-oriented land allocation procedures.

"Agreement between USAID and the Oblast of Nizhni Novgorod for Technical Assistance in the Housing Sector"
Signed: 7/94.
Agreed by:
B. Nemtsov, Governor, Oblast of Nizhni Novgorod;
J. Norris, Director, USAID, Russian Federation.
Period of Performance: 2 years.
The principal areas for mutual work and assistance to the oblast by American and Russian experts are: (1) To work with the Nizhni Novgorod Academy of Architecture and Construction to develop courses during 1994 in housing economics and the economics of investment decisions in housing construction.

(2) To provide expert review of documents prepared by the oblast of housing reform, including rent reform, housing finance, and housing maintenance activities.

(3) To work with the oblast on design and implementation of its program for raising rents and introducing housing allowances.

(4) To work with the oblast administration to determine its appropriate role in fostering the development of a housing finance system in the oblast and to work with a bank in the oblast to begin long-term mortgage lending on market principles.

Table A.1 CHRONOLOGY OF URBAN INSTITUTE WORK ON HOUSING SECTOR REFORM PROGRAM UNDER USAID CONTRACTS—
USAID/RUSSIAN FEDERATION AND USAID/REGIONAL ADMINISTRATION AGREEMENTS: NOVEMBER 1991–MARCH 1996
(continued)

Stages of program identification and implementation	USAID/UI contracts	Agreements between USAID and the Russian Federation	Agreements between USAID and regional and municipal governments
			"Memorandum of Understanding between USAID and the Municipality of St. Petersburg for Shelter Sector Reform." Signed: 3/23/95. *Agreed by:* V. Yakovlev, Head of Municipal Administration of City of St. Petersburg; J. Norris, Director, USAID, Russian Federation. *Period of Performance: 3/23/95–09/30/96. Principal areas of cooperation will be in the development of new relationships in the housing sector and land market:* (1) Establishment of procedures for registration of condominiums; support to homeowners associations leading to improved management and maintenance of housing stock. (2) Development of procedures for procuring of housing management and maintenance services by competitive bidding. (3) Reduction of housing subsidies through a rational housing allowance program.

HSRP II
implementation
October 1995–present

"Housing Sector
Reform Project II"
Signed: 9/28/95.
Period of Performance:
10/1/95–09/30/97.
Main tasks: Housing
finance, infrastructure
finance, enterprise
housing divestiture
projects in four cities
(Ryazan, Vladimir,
Moscow, Nizhni
Novgorod oblast)

None

(4) Development of rational housing
finance systems supported by both public
and private sectors.

Agreements for Technical Assistance in
Housing Sector between USAID and:
(1) The Oblast Administration of Nizhni
Novgorod, signed 3/12/96.
(2) The City of Moscow, signed 4/25/96.
(3) The City of Vladimir, signed 2/22/96.
(4) The City of Ryazan, signed 2/29/96.
Period of Performance: 2 years, with
assistance concentrated during the first 12
months.
The main directions of work:
(a) Infrastructure finance (rationalization
of fees for communal services;
mechanisms for long-term financing of
infrastructure investments).
(b) Enterprise housing divestiture and
work with local administration with
received stock (promotion of units
privatization, formation of condominium
associations, introducing competitive
maintenance).
(c) Work with banks on housing finance
(mortgage loans, construction period
finance).[a]
(d) Work with developers on construction
finance and infrastructure finance
projects.[a]

a. Vladimir is not participating in this element.

During the Moscow trip, Struyk also met with various federal and municipal representatives regarding the prospects for collaboration (including Gosstroi of Russia and the Moscow Department of Municipal Housing); established initial contacts with potential Russian consultants in addition to Kosareva; and further evaluated the scope of housing sector problems in Russia. Struyk also participated in an international meeting in Moscow organized by the Ministry of Architecture, Construction, and Housing Maintenance of Russia (now the Ministry of Construction of Russia) and the U.S. National Association of Home Builders. The "USAID team" was led by Peter Kimm, USAID representative and director of the agency's Office of Housing and Urban Programs, and included Struyk.

During January and February 1992, the Russian consultant Kosareva, as requested by The Urban Institute, both organized meetings with representatives of the interested federal and municipal governments of three cities—Moscow, Ekaterinburg, and Novosibirsk[1]—which USAID had by then selected as the primary locations for its housing reform work, and collected initial statistical data on the state of the housing sector in Russian and in the selected cities. In March 1992 a mission comprising two representatives from The Urban Institute (including Struyk), consultant Kosareva, and an interpreter spent three weeks in the three cities Moscow, Novosibirsk, and Ekaterinburg, identifying, at the federation and city levels, potential partners from governmental structures and discussing with them specific directions for technical assistance in housing reform (the latter was guided by a range of options in a "menu" of possible activities defined by USAID).

Key partners from the Russian side were quickly identified: at the federal level, Minstroi, the Ministry of Economy, and the Working Center on Economic Reform of the Russian Federation; and at the Moscow Municipal level, the Department of Municipal Housing and the Department of Engineering Support (the latter of which provides public utilities such as district heat, water, gas, and maintenance services). To avoid over-dependence on a single ministry or department, several interested partners from the Russian side were identified. Subsequent program implementation confirmed the validity of such an approach, although the leading roles were initially assumed by one or two Russian partners (Minstroi of Russia and the Finance Ministry at the federation level, and the Department of Engineering Support in Moscow).

As a result of these collaborative meetings, as well as the emphasis paid to defining directions for technical assistance and new housing policies that would complement the conditions in Russia, a two-year agreement was readily signed with the Russian Federation and the City of Moscow, following the conclusion of the three-week mission, with the cities of Novosibirsk and Ekaterinburg signing somewhat later (see table A.1).

Initial Collaboration

Discussions with the Russian side identified the following priorities for initial collaboration in the housing sphere at the Russian Federation level (see table A.1):

- Elaboration of the legal and regulatory bases for transforming the housing sector to a market-based operation and reforming the system of town-planning regulations; and
- Formation of a system of housing finance, including developing the legal base and creating mechanisms (lending procedures, loan instruments) for long-term mortgage lending to the public.

Defining the main housing reform directions and providing the legal basis for their realization required, first of all, working with executive and legislative authorities at the federal level. (Even now, the regulating role of the federal authorities is difficult to overestimate; despite that in accordance with the new 1993 Constitution, housing legislation is under the joint authority of the Russian Federation and the Subjects of the Russian Federation, the greater part of the social housing stock (49.7 percent) is under municipal ownership, and its management is exclusively the province of municipalities.) Few regions take initiative in conducting housing reform (the exceptions being Nizhni Novgorod *oblast* (region), Krasnoyarsk krai, cities of Moscow, Ryazan, and some others). Most of the regions, recognizing the potentially strong social reaction to a radical housing reform, prefer to go along with reforms dictated by the federal level. This trend was even more pronounced at the initial stage of reform.

Regarding formation of a system of housing finance in Russia, this issue was also given top priority not only because of the acuteness of the problem but also because its resolution was hindered by economic and legislative concerns and by a lack of qualified personnel. It was anticipated that The Urban Institute would participate in preparing the necessary legal and normative requirements and would recommend specific operations related to long-term mortgage housing lending, including elaboration of a loan instrument structured for high and volatile inflation rates, the means of attracting funds for lending, underwriting and loan servicing techniques, and so forth.

Improvement of the management system and maintenance of the municipal housing stock were identified as priorities for cooperation by the two main Moscow housing committees (i.e., the Department of Engineering Support—formerly the Moscow Engineering Committee—which oversees the maintenance and repair of the housing stock; and the Department of Municipal Housing—formerly the Moscow Housing Committee—which was in charge of allocation and privatization of the housing stock. Plans were made for a pilot project illustrating the effects of hiring maintenance firms on a competitive basis in one of the city's administrative districts. The first project was later implemented in the Zapadny district and the prefect of this district confirmed the agreement with USAID, publicly committing himself to the experiment.

The March 1992 housing sector agreements provided for the possibility of expanding the scope of work subject to the mutual consent of the parties. In practice, various features were added as the Russian side came to recognize the severity of specific problems and the value of the technical assistance by American and Russian experts.

During the life of the Housing Sector Reform Program, its activities involved the participation, on a fairly permanent basis, of a large number of regions (over 20), commercial banks (over 25), and other organizations. However, special agreements between USAID and a cooperating partner were signed only when close (almost weekly) interaction was planned. Some agreements were also made by The Urban Institute at the request of partners—for example, with small regional cities for limited cooperation programs. In general, the signing of formal agreements often had little impact on the intensity of activity from the viewpoint of the city.

For the purpose of creating practical mechanisms for mortgage lending to individuals, a two-year agreement was signed in November 1992 with one of Russia's largest banks—Mosbusinessbank. The agreement provided for developing mortgage lending procedures by adapting international practices to Russian conditions, and included all components of the mortgage lending process, from loan underwriting to developing a loan instrument that would both have acceptable risk to the bank and be affordable to the borrower under high and volatile inflation conditions.

At the end of the first two-year term agreement, the Russian Federation and the City of Moscow signed two new agreements in July 1994 (see table A.1). These stipulated continuing collaboration for another two years in ongoing areas of work. The first of these new agreements provided for continuing formation of the legal and normative base of housing reform, development of long-term mortgage lending, privatization of housing maintenance, housing payments reform; deeper cooperation in certain directions (creation of condominiums); and new activities (demonstration projects on developing a mechanism for the competitive allocation of municipal land plots.

The second agreement provided for expanded collaboration with specific regions of the Russian Federation. In 1994–1995 comprehensive reform agreements were made with the Nizhni Novgorod oblast and the City of Saint-Petersburg to pursue cooperation programs nearly identical to the work being carried out by The Urban Institute in Moscow. Presented with an example of a successful start at housing reform, these other regions were eager, at least at the negotiating stage,[2] to obtain similar results. Within the framework of this second agreement, The Urban Institute also began working in numerous other regions of the Russian Federation, primarily on such issues as privatization of maintenance of municipal housing, creation of condominiums, reform of rent levels, and implementation of the housing allowance program. Urban Institute consultants were involved in the same housing activities that had been under the "economic control" of enterprises and had then been divested to municipalities under Russia's industrial privatization program.

Stages of Program Implementation

Implementation of a large-scale, complex program of technical assistance to reform any sector of the economy (such as the HSRP) may be arbitrarily divided into three stages:

1. Launching of the program, including demonstration projects in an initial region or commercial entity;
2. Expanding the demonstration projects over a wider, though still limited, number of regions and commercial entities; and
3. Transition from a few demonstration projects to achieve a general reform.

The course of the housing sector cooperation program closely followed the scheme just described (see table A.1). During the four years of its implementation, activities to inaugurate a new housing policy and the supporting legal and normative frameworks were carried on continuously at the level of Russian Federation and regional governments. Meanwhile the number and types of demonstration projects were gradually expanded.

STAGE ONE: 1992–1993

The first stage of implementing the housing sector cooperation program covered the years 1992–93 (table A.2). During this period, activities concentrated mainly on elaborating at the Russian Federation level the concept of a new housing policy and its legal base; inaugurating two demonstration projects with the City of Moscow (reform of the rental payments system and introduction of the housing allowances program, as well as an alternative approach to maintaining the municipal housing stock); and intensive collaboration with Mosbusinessbank to develop long-term residential mortgage lending. At the request of the head of the Working Center for Economic Reform of the Russian Federation (WCER), an in-depth analysis was conducted by The Urban Institute of the funding crisis in the state and municipal housing stock. The problem was acute not only because of the extreme budget problems presented by the then-current housing operations but because of the general price liberalization accompanied by high inflation in Russia and the continued policy (unchanged since 1928) of restricting rent increases.

The Urban Institute thus proposed a program of gradually increasing residents' rents up to 100 percent coverage with a simultaneous introduction of housing allowances, i.e., income-tested subsidies for low-income households. Although the Institute's initial plans included only a demonstration project in Moscow, the proposal was soon adopted by all of Russia and was included as one provision in the law "On the Foundations of the Federal Housing Policy" (December 1992). As such, it constituted a major step toward intial implementation of the HSRP in Russia.

This demonstration phase also included a pilot project in Moscow's Zapadny district to illustrate the feasibility and efficiency of maintaining the municipal housing stock by competitively selected private companies. Whereas initially the demonstration project covered 2,000 apartments, by December 1995 some 10 percent of the housing stock in Moscow (325,000 units) was maintained by this method.

During its first six months the program achieved substantial results, both in helping to create the legal base for implementating housing reform, as well as in developing the overall housing reform concept. This blueprint was experimentally confirmed and then finally adopted on a mass scale. Its facets included:

Table A.2 GROWTH OF USAID/URBAN INSTITUTE SHELTER COOPERATION PROGRAM IN RUSSIA BY TASKS AND BY REGIONS AND BANKS, 1992–1996

Program stages[a]	Beginning date	Additional work tasks	Additional regions and banks[b]
First Stage	1992	Housing policy Housing legislation Housing rent reform and housing allowances program Privatization of housing maintenance	Russian Federation Moscow
	1993	+ Housing mortgage lending	Mosbusinessbank
Second Stage	1994	+ Condominiums creation + Up-front subsidies program for housing construction and purchases	+ Nizhni Novgorod oblast + 10 cities or regions + 10 banks
	January 1995	+ Enterprise housing divestiture + Land auctions for housing construction + Urban land zoning	+ St. Petersburg + 10 cities or regions + 10 banks
Third Stage	October 1995	+ Housing construction finance + Infrastructure finance	+ 4 cities + 5 banks

a. See description in text.
b. For the prior work tasks or new tasks.

- Privatization of the state and municipal housing stock;
- Introduction of real rights to private ownership of housing;
- Reform of the payment system for social rental housing;
- Demonopolization and privatization of the housing maintenance sector;
- Introduction of targeted (based on income and other factors) programs to support payments for rental housing and for construction and purchase of housing.

Although a complex of interconnected factors determined the success of this critical, initial stage of the program, the main determinants were as follows:

1. The acuteness of the housing sector crisis and the readiness of the Russian side to consider necessary reforms;
2. The program's ability to provide a comprehensive system for the new housing policy adequate to Russia's current situation;
3. The intensive involvement of program consultants with government counterparts in the legislative process, thus permitting the timely development of regulations and other legal requirements;
4. The program's initiative in proposing specific options, supported whenever necessary by the appropriate calculations and modeling.[3]

Stage Two: 1994–September 1995

The second stage—1994 to September 1995—was characterized by program expansion in a number of areas, including creation of condominiums in multifamily buildings; development of a scheme for downpayment subsidies for purchase and construction of housing to citizens officially defined as needing improved living conditions; tendering land plots for housing construction and regulating the use of urban land; and beginning to address issues related to divestiture of the enterprise housing stock to municipalities.

In 1995 the World Bank began appraisals of a loan project aimed at facilitating acceptance by the Russian municipalities of the housing stock from enterprises that had been divested as part of the privatization process. Prior to the economic reforms, about 40 percent of the housing stock was in the possession of state ministries, departments, institutions, and enterprises. Privatization of enterprises initiated a mass "unloading" of this social burden from enterprises onto the municipalities. It was expected that this process could be facilitated by:

- Lower subsidies to maintain the housing stock (through increasing tenant payments and introduction of housing allowances);
- Enhanced financial and economic effectiveness of management and housing operations (through privatization of apartments, creation of condominiums, and demonopolizing of management and maintenance activities); and
- Lower housing utilities costs (through better heat insulation of residential buildings and introduction of energy-efficient techniques for other utilities).

It was planned to allocate the World Bank funds toward energy-efficient retrofitting of buildings. Regarding the first two directions, provisions were made for technical assistance to design and implement appropriate actions. Through an agreement between the World Bank and USAID, The Urban Institute was assigned to these activities for five cities (Vladimir, Ryazan, Volkhov, Petrozavodsk, and Novocherkassk).

In September 1995 The Urban Institute won the second USAID contract for technical assistance in housing reform in Russia. The project primarily involved intensive activities in four selected localities (Moscow, Ryazan, Vladimir, Nizhni Novgorod oblast) in specified areas, namely:

- Long-term finance infrastructure;
- Enterprise housing divesture, including privatization of apartments, creation of homeowners associations, and competitive selection of maintenance companies; and
- Development of financial institutions' housing lending programs (mortgage loans for housing purchase and loans to developers for housing construction).

As it turned out, the localities selected did not always show equal interest along these lines. Thus, for example, commercial banks in Vladimir were unprepared to begin loan organizations for purchase or construction of housing. Consequently, the agreement signed with that city does not provide for working with banks and building companies to develop housing lending. At the same time, officials in Moscow have been unable for a number of reasons to accelerate changes in the city's system for financing infrastructure investments; however, while recognizing the importance of housing divestiture, the city considers it necessary to adopt a diversified approach to its municipal housing stock, irrespective of its ownership history. Because of this position, the Moscow agreement includes only one pilot project (using the "Vodokanal" water company) on developing a new approach to infrastructure finance, while continuing joint activities in the maintenance reform and management of municipal housing, including divested enterprise stock. The experiences of these cities illustrate the importance of consulting with the party receiving technical assistance at an early point in the project's design, to ensure maximum interest and cooperation during implementation.

The 1994–95 period was marked by considerable reform activity within the Nizhni Novgorod oblast and the City of Saint-Petersburg. In five cities (Vladimir, Ryazan, Volkhov, Petrozavodsk, Novocherkassk)—all potential borrowers under the World Bank loan to improve energy-saving systems in residential buildings—cooperation was begun to reform the rental payments system, demonopolize the housing maintenance sector, and privatize the management of the housing stock by creating condominiums. About 15 other regions and 20 commerical banks participated in the cooperation program on a less-intensive but permanent basis.

Dissemination of project results—a crucial aspect of the project— was achieved mainly by organizing seminars and training courses through Russian public professional associations (Association of Mortgage Banks, Russian Guild of Realtors, etc.), as well as educational institutions (e.g., International Academy of Entrepreneurs), and the massive distribution of low-cost guidelines, manuals, and other documents.

STAGE THREE: OCTOBER 1995–1996

The third stage (October 1995 through 1996) inaugurated a radical change in the program structure. The main goal was defined as transition from a few demonstration projects to a steady process of relevant reforms in the housing sector. To achieve this purpose, it was necessary to shift from a horizontal geographical expansion of reform to wider-scale reforms in specified regions. In other words, there was a shift from maximizing the number of partner cities to deepening reforms in cities in which the project was already working. During this period, therefore, few new cities or regions have been attracted to the program, and every effort has been made to strengthen the achieved reforms in all partner regions in order to gain results in all areas of reform. At the time of this writing (March 1996), the program is in the middle of this third stage, which is projected to last through 1996.

SELECTED PROGRAM COMPONENTS

This section examines five key aspects in the operation of the Housing Sector Reform Program. These aspects, which tend to assume different priorities at different stages of program implementation (see table A.2) include:

1. *Development of the reform concept and its inclusion in legal and regulatory documents* at the appropriate levels of government (federation, federation subject, or municipality)—in other words, *creation of a legal base* for implementing the planned activities.
2. *Implementation of demonstration projects,* which illustrate in practice the possibility and effectiveness of the reforms.
3. *Continuous monitoring and evaluation* of the progress and results of the demonstration projects; comparison with the initial or alternative systems, if necessary; modeling and forecasting of effects of different decisions; and summarizing the actual results.
4. *Dissemination of results* of successful demonstration projects to other regional and economic entities. Dissemination requires a specific mechanism that includes development and distribution of methodologies and materials for implementation of relevant projects, professional training of specialists, creation of information channels to publicize the experience, and so on.
5. *Institutionalization* of the reforms and/or mechanisms for their development; and introduction and replication of programs, including training to ensure continuity of the reform process beyond the technical assistance phase.

Legal Support of Reform

Activities to create a legal base for housing and urban planning reform were carried out at all stages of the Housing Sector Reform Program, though, of course, this aspect received greater stress during stages one and two, when it was necessary both to provide a reform basis at the federal level and to adopt the necessary documents to support every demonstration project at the local or regional level. However, the legislative process is the least controlled and least predictable process, with success dependent on a multitude of primarily political factors.

As noted, at the first stage of program implementation, program consultants helped to draft the law "On the Foundations of the Federal

Housing Policy" (passed in December 1992), as well as the law "On the Foundations of the Urban Planning Policy" (passed in May 1993), which provided the minimum necessary bases for the housing and urban planning reforms. In later phases of the program, consultants participated in drafting the following laws: "On Mortgage," "On Associations of Home Owners," "Housing Codes," "Town-Planning Code," and "Law on Territorial Zoning." As of March 1996 these proposed laws are at different stages in the legislative process. The program's consultants also helped to draft numerous legal and enabling documents at the federal level (Presidential Decrees, government resolutions, ministry and department resolutions) on issues pertaining to housing finance, creation of condominiums, reform of the rent system, and other topics (see table A.2).

Demonstration Projects

In addition to legal support, the other key element—if not the most important element—of technical assistance in the reform process is demonstration projects. Naturally, a successful demonstration project may not always lead to widespread reform. However, it constitutes a strong argument in its favor. By the same token, even if a negative result is obtained, the cost of the experiment is usually negligible compared to the experience gained.

The Urban Institute, primarily at the first and second stages, successfully implemented a large number of demonstration projects related chiefly to:

- Increasing payments for rent and utilities by the population and providing housing allowances to low-income citizens, beginning with detailed design work in Moscow in 1993 and, since January 1994, becoming operational first in several cities of Central Russia and then quickly over the whole of Russia.
- Competitions among private contractors to maintain the municipal housing stock. The first competition was held in Moscow in March 1993 for maintenance of 2,000 municipal apartments by private contractors; by the end of 1995, 10 percent of Moscow's housing stock was being serviced under similar arrangments. Corresponding experiments were also successful in Ryazan, Novocherkassk, Nizhni Novgorod, Vladimir, and a number of other cities and regions.
- Creation of condominiums with transfer of management functions to them (assistance was provided in the formation of condominiums

in 10 Russian cities, including Novocherkassk, Ryazan, Nizhni Novgorod, Vladimir, Ivanovo, Volgograd, and others).

- Making long-term mortgage loans for the purchase of housing. Mosbusinessbank was one of the first Russian banks to originate such loans to its employees, in May 1994. As of March 1996, about 15 banks had some experience in long-term residential mortgage lending to the public, and about 10 others were to begin such operations in the near future.
- Lending for housing construction. The Urban Institute consulted with 14 banks in March 1996, primarily to delineate and refine procedures for loan underwriting and loan dispersal.
- Providing subsidies for purchase and construction of housing to military service personnel. In 1993 The Urban Institute developed and implemented in the cities of Pskov, Novgorod, and Yaroslavl a housing voucher scheme for retired military officers from the Baltic states; vouchers could be used to purchase a unit in the open market, and funds came from an American grant. In fall of 1994, a similar scheme of providing up-front subsidies to those on waiting lists with federal funds was tested for the first time with 700 certificates in Nizhni Novgorod oblast.
- Organizing auctions of plots of land allocated for residential construction (the first auctions were held in fall 1995 in the cities of Tver and Nizhni Novgorod, some within the framework of the World Bank residential construction loan).

Monitoring and Evaluation

The value of monitoring and evaluation activities within the Housing Sector Reform Program cannot be overestimated. Four major components of evaluation were utilized in various aspects of the Housing Sector Reform Program by The Urban Institute.

First, to determine the effectiveness of the demonstration projects, the Institute conducted surveys of program participants. In one such survey, Muscovites residing in municipal buildings were interviewed prior to transfer of building maintenance to a competitively selected private company, and then again after the new firm had been on the job for several months.[4] Comparison of the survey results revealed increased quality of housing maintenance with the private company. Periodic surveys were also done in Vladimir and Gorodets, cities that were among the first to launch the rent reform and to provide housing allowances to low-income households. A 1994 survey revealed insufficient information to the public on the existence of the housing allow-

ances programs and a corresponding low program participation in
both cities. On the other hand, participants in both cities reported
being well treated by administrators and the process of enrolling was
found to be efficient. An evaluation in 1995 found knowledge and
participation rates at much higher levels, although some administrative problems emerged (Struyk, Puzanov, and Lee 1996).

The second major component involves The Urban Institute's monitoring of its activities in a variety of spheres, including updating
information on: the state of housing lending among commercial banks
that cooperate with the Institute; competitions for maintenance of the
housing stock; the number of created condominiums; the parameters
of rent reform in regions and cities; and the extent of participation in
the housing allowances program.

A third major evaluation component involves efforts by The Urban
Institute to collect and summarize data on overall developments in
the HSRP. Thus, using the Goskomstat data (form "ZKH" 22) as well
as Urban Institute's own data on regions, the database on the status
of rent reform in Russia is periodically updated and advisory information distributed to program administrators (see Puzanov 1996, for
example).

As another example, the process of condominium formation in Russia and introduction of competitive selection of housing maintenance
companies are monitored through periodic semiannual collection of
information from about 40 regions with which the Institute has either
close ties or periodic contacts at seminars, meetings, and similar
events.

In addition, a telephone survey of real estate companies and banks
that participated in the housing lending process was conducted to
monitor the progress of "housing sale by installment"—a long-term
mortgage lending instrument that is new for Russia but has been
widely used because the legal base for mortgage lending is currently
rather weak. It should be noted that the information developed by the
project—although often fragmentary—is often the only source regarding market-based transformations in the housing sector, and as such
is useful to governmental bodies.

The fourth and final evaluation component involved periodic surveys and analyses of a wider spectrum of indicators to estimate the
overall pace and trends of housing reform, as well as development of
the housing market nationally and in Moscow (the most advanced
region in terms of market-based transformations). Thus, during 1989–
94, more than 50 housing indicators were collected and analyzed on
an average for Russia and for Moscow, using the calculations based

on the UNCHS/World Bank/USAID methodology (all, for example, Pchelintsev, Belkina, and Tcherbakova 1994). These indicators document the general trends in housing; the volume and forms of housing construction; financial sources; and demographic, economic, and financial indicators.

Panel surveys were conducted in Moscow in 1992, 1993, 1994, and 1995, covering about 2,500 apartments randomly selected from the entire housing stock. The same apartments were included each year, with a sample of newly constructed apartments added annually (Lee and Romanik 1995). The surveys were designed to analyze housing market dynamics, population mobility and the volume of housing transactions, and housing expense burdens, among other factors.

At the end of 1993 and the beginning of 1994, The Urban Institute conducted household surveys similar to those done in Moscow in each of the seven cities that were candidates to participate in the World Bank loan to develop residential housing construction. The cities were Moscow, Saint-Petersburg, Tver, Rostov-on-Don, Novgorod, Nizhni Novgorod, and Barnaul. Three other surveys were also conducted in the cities. Together these efforts included: surveys of developers who offer newly constructed housing for sale; surveys of households to determine housing conditions, residential mobility, and housing preferences as well as demand; collections of statistical data from real estate brokers on transactions (prices, unit attributes) in the housing market; compilations of housing sector indicators, described earlier. The information collected in the seven cities included more than 7,600 interviews with households, data on 231 residential development projects, and 3,432 transactions on housing sales. At the time, the data represented, in essence, the only readily available source of systematic information on the emerging Russian housing market.[5]

Dissemination

The importance of dissemination activities increased dramatically with the appearance of the first positive results from the demonstration projects. The HSRP demonstrates that under current conditions in Russia, the following types of dissemination activities are particularly effective:

- Preparation and dissemination of methodological materials and booklets;
- Publications and presentations in the mass media, and publication of scientific papers; and

- Training courses, seminars, meetings, and lectures organized by program consultants (project brochures are disseminated at such presentations).

The forms providing maximum coverage with broad mass appeal are publications and presentations in the mass media and—to some extent—scientific papers. The HSRP used these forms for wide-scale public dissemination of the basic ideas and concepts of housing reform, and as information resources during consultations at both the national and regional levels. For example, The Urban Institute provides information on condominium formation in a column in the Moscow monthly newspaper *Khvartirier*.

Collaboration with the mass media has both positive and negative aspects, and the HSRP, rather than aggressively seeking out the media, has more often responded to requests from them for interviews or information. On the positive side, informed media analysis can have a widespread, beneficial social effect. On the other hand, in Russia's current climate, it is also important to be sensitive to reports of reforms vis-à-vis descriptions of technical assistance; in practice this has usually meant focusing on the reforms themselves and deemphasizing the roles of outsiders.

Publication of analyses of the HSRP in scientific journals (e.g., *Voprosy ekonomiki, Ekonomikomatematicheskie metody, EKO*) and in professional journals and newspapers (*Dengi i kredit, Stroitelnaya gazeta, Ipoteka,* and others) has allowed for discussion of proposed ideas among a broad professional and scientific audience. These publications also served to introduce the program to this audience as a formal, institutional unit, thus gaining acceptance for it.

Major emphasis was also given to preparing and disseminating booklets, brochures, and printed materials on different aspects of the housing reform and the program's activities. As of March 1996, more than 80 such titles had been distributed in the form of mass mailings to interested individuals and organizations cooperating with the program; dissemination of materials at all seminars, meetings, training courses, and lectures organized by The Urban Institute or its specialists, or at related events held by other organizations (e.g., Union of Russian Cities, Association of Mortgage Banks, and so forth); providing selected materials to all interested organizations and persons on a regular basis.

The most effective dissemination tactic, however, seems to be distribution of materials among professional audiences specifically engaged in solving a targeted problem. Methodological materials describing in detail the process of organizing and introducing specific mechanisms into practice were prepared for nearly every program direction on the basis of generalized results of demonstration projects or as formal aspects of training courses. Through February 1996 the program prepared 25 such guidebooks or manuals, of which 11 deal with bank housing lending, 5 with the housing allowance program, and 9 with the creation and functioning of condominiums, organizing the competition to select firms for maintaining municipal housing, and supervising such firms during the contract period.

Most of the initial methodological materials on housing lending were prepared in conjunction with the technical assistance rendered to Mosbusinessbank on introducing long-term mortgage lending for housing purchase. A series of nine issues was produced, including manuals on loan origination and servicing, legal support of lending, alternative loan instruments, pricing loans, loan underwriting, and so forth. After program consultants developed the software for servicing loans originated with different instruments, a book, *Description of Software for Servicing Mortgage Loans* (including a set of diskettes), was prepared and published. These materials were disseminated exclusively among banking professionals. Unlike the booklets or other printed matter for the wider public, which were distributed free of charge, these strictly professional materials were often distributed through professional unions such as the Association of Mortgage Banks and the Association of Commerical Banks "Russia," which, under agreement with The Urban Institute, could set a price for these materials to compensate for the expenses of dissemination.

Sometimes methodological materials prepared by The Urban Institute were published jointly by the appropriate governmental administration, ministry, or department. Thus, for example, materials on the housing allowance program, which are used by almost every local housing allowance agency in the country, were distributed as recommendations of the Ministry of Construction of the Russian Federation. (Official support is tremendously important when a state or municipal program is being implemented.)

Training courses, seminars, and meetings are also important vehicles for information dissemination. The Housing Sector Reform Program's policy was always either to team up with other Russian groups who handled the technical details of such events or for project staff to make presentations at events held by other Russian organizations. The Urban Institute's principal partner on the issue of housing lending was the Association of Mortgage Banks, with whom 14 professional training courses were offered in 1993–95. Lectures consisted of both American program consultants and Russian specialists. The courses were offered both in Moscow and in regions that invited and helped to sponsor the courses. Similar cooperation took place with the Association of Commercial Banks "Russia," the Guild of Realtors, and other organizations.

The principal partner with The Urban Institute for training courses on reform of rental payments and the operation and management of housing was the International Academy of Entrepreneurs, with whom five courses were offered in 1994–95. The program also cooperated with the Institute for Housing and Communal Economy on some conferences.

In addition, one- or two-day seminars in cities or regions were widely conducted at the invitation of the respective administrations. About 50 such seminars were presented by The Urban Institute during 1993–95.

Through 1995 more than 250,000 copies of different publications had been distributed, and more than 100 training courses, seminars, and presentations had been conducted in the course of the HSRP's implementation. This dissemination program was highly effective and in many cases provided information sufficient for a local administration or banker to begin a new activity with no follow-up assistance required.

Institutionalization

Institutionalization of the program is perhaps the most difficult element to implement. Its purpose is to create mechanisms to ensure, at a minimum, that reforms continue after technical assistance terminates and, at a maximum, to establish institutions that could, in time, independently develop and implement new directions within their respective economic and social policy spheres.

In the course of program assistance in the HSRP, the main directions toward institutionalization may be identified as:

1. Forming or identifying a local administrative structure that would be responsible for continuing the activities that were performed by The Urban Institute during the demonstration projects;
2. Attracting Russian institutes to organize training courses (such courses must be both of inherent interest and profitable to the institutes);
3. Assisting in forming and developing professional associations interested in protecting and supporting specified reforms; and

4. Offering assistance and support to a Russian institute that would assume to a certain degree the functions of assisting with housing reform—operating on market-based principles—after termination of the program.

Within the framework of the first direction, success of a transition from demonstration projects to mass reforms has always depended on the transfer of implementation, dissemination, and training functions to the local structures. An example is provided by the Moscow project on competitions for maintenance of the municipal housing stock by private companies, currently implemented by the Department of Engineering Support of Moscow and the Unified Customer Services (DEZ) of the municipal districts that contract for maintenance of the municipal stock in their regions. The competitions are now self-sustaining, and training of the DEZ employees is carried out by a private firm. By 1996, The Urban Institute's functions consisted of periodic consultations and development of a new demonstration project involving selection of a firm to manage (as opposed to maintain) the housing stock—the next step in the reform of the city's housing operation.

One example of institutionalization of an entire reform element is a network of housing allowance agencies created at the local level nearly nationwide. By summer 1995, such agencies administered the programs covering 95 percent of all households. The presence of such a broad network of agencies with ability to provide social assistance based on household income (housing allowances are the unique national income-tested program) makes it possible to use these agencies as a base for implementing income-dependent social support programs on a wider scale.

Regarding the second direction of institutionalization, when attempting to attract Russian institutions to training courses and seminars, it is very important to be aware that such institutions operate on market principles. They will never be able to define the market demand for such training so long as consumers are offered a free product through technical assistance program subsidies.

With respect to financing training courses organized through Russian entities (Association of Mortgage Banks, International Academy of Entrepreneurs, etc.), the HSRP has always adhered to the principle of self-sufficiency and profitability of the courses to such organizations. It should be noted, however, that the market demand did not fully coincide with the curriculum offered by The Urban Institute. In such cases the Institute's partners tried (not always successfully) to meet the perceived demand, which sometimes resulted in lower-quality courses, and a dilution of the training focus. In such cases the Institute had to seek contacts with new partners having a more aggressive and subtler marketing policy. Sometimes, when for a number of objective reasons there was no effective demand for a topic, yet training was essential for the demonstration projects, the Institute conducted training at its own expense.

The HSRP's support of a newly created professional union is demonstrated by its cooperation with the Association of Mortgage Banks, which was created in 1993 and had 24 members in early 1996. The association's members are commercial banks and real estate and construction companies interested in developing mortgage business. The Urban Institute assisted the association in defining the course of its development, framing its policies to attract members, and organizing a training program to support its activities. It should be noted that lack of a legal base for the mortgage lending, economic conditions that are unfavorable to long-term lending, and a reserved approach to attracting new members have militated against the association being an active and influential public banking organization.

In terms of a successor to The Urban Institute's program, the institutionalization process took a natural course owing to the Institute's policy of attracting predominantly Russian specialists to implement the program. After three to four years of intensive program activity, these Russian specialists have been highly trained in the development of housing policy, housing finance, implementation of demonstration projects in the housing sector, and analysis and evaluation of results. To preserve the team of specialists formed during this time, and to create a basis for accumulating experience in the future, a Russian Institute for Urban Economics was founded in November 1995. Established by six leading specialists in the Housing Sector Reform Program, the Russian Institute's principal activities consist of defining and analyzing the social and economic problems of the urban territories, developing mechanisms for their solution, and assisting in their practical implementation. The Institute is an independent, nonprofit organization whose board of trustees includes prominent scientists and administrative figures in fields consistent with the Institute's work, as well as representatives of private and public organizations, including a representative from The Urban Institute.

In early 1996, the Russian Institute was engaged in the Housing Sector Reform Program under subcontract to The Urban Institute (U.S.). The new Institute's strategy through 1997 will be to build on its experience through work with other potential clients, as well as to concentrate on the further development of the Institute itself, in order to form a stable base for activities upon termination of the USAID program.

ORGANIZATIONAL ISSUES IN PROGRAM IMPLEMENTATION

Personnel Policy and Support of Program Activities

In the four years of its operations to date, the Housing Sector Reform Program has both increased its personnel and shifted the proportions of Russian–U.S. staff. Between May 1992 and May 1996, the number of permanent and temporary professional consultants increased from 4 to 39 (see table A.3), not counting administrative personnel and translators (which amount to about 25 percent of the number of consultants). A further increase to 52 specialists is planned to accompany

Table A.3 URBAN INSTITUTE HOUSING SECTOR REFORM PROGRAM PROFESSIONAL STAFF LEVELS IN RUSSIA, MAY 1992–MAY 1996

Date	Russian	Long-term U.S.[a]	Short-term U.S.[b]
1992: May	1	1	2
September	2	2	2
1993: May	4	2	2
September	5	3	3
1994: May	10	3	3
September	14	5	3
1995: May	17	5	2
September[c]	20	5	3
1996: May	32[d]	4	3
September[e]	44[f]	3	5

a. Long-term U.S. staff from September 1993 to summer 1996 includes an intern/research assistant working on monitoring and evaluation tasks.
b. Figures for short-term advisors are averages for spring or fall seasons, but full-time equivalents are somewhat less.
c. Start of implementation of second contract to The Urban Institute under the Housing Sector Reform Program. It is expected to operate concurrently with the first contract until summer 1997.
d. Includes 15 professionals employed by the Russian Institute for Urban Economics under contract to The Urban Institute.
e. Start of work on four additional task orders under the second contract. Figure is an estimate.
f. Includes 22 professionals employed by the Russian Institute for Urban Economics. Figure is an estimate.

the projected extension of the program in summer and autumn of 1996.

The main elements of the program's personnel policy are the following:

1. Priority has been given to attracting Russian specialists for principal activities involving adapting program concepts to the Russian situation; practical implementation of projects; training; and dissemination of results. Highly qualified specialists with an economic, legal, geographic, or financial background were sought. Preference was given to those with experience in the housing sector. However, because a limited number of such specialists was available, professionals specializing in related fields were also employed (construction, architecture, regional economics, town planning, and sociology). Whereas the number of Russian specialists has grown steadily during the life of the program, the number of resident American consultants to it, having passsed its maximum in September 1995 (five persons), is to be reduced to two by March 1997. The average number of American consultants invited on a short-term basis has remained stable at two to three persons.

2. A maximum effort has been made to create stability and continuity in the positions held by American advisors. Key examples are Steven Butler, the project's Legal Advisor since the fall of 1992, and Gene Rizor, who assisted with the development of the housing allowance program.

3. Gradual transfer of a great number of functions to Russian personnel. At the program's start, management functions (excluding the Russian-side manager of the program), as well as project development, were carried out mainly by American specialists or under their guidance. However, starting in fall 1995, most of these functions were reassigned to the Russian specialists. Beginning in summer 1996, when the number of resident American participants will have been reduced to three persons, it is planned that middle management (responsible for implementing projects and personnel relations) will mainly be represented by Russians. United States specialists, invited as consultants, will develop new projects and work with their Russian counterparts to introduce and integrate the projects, including preparing methodological materials.

4. Recruitment of Russian specialists was on a permanent basis. Certain Russian consultants or scientific research firms were contracted with temporarily to fulfill specific tasks (e.g., conducting

surveys or other short-term projects) not involving the everyday activities of the program.

5. Whenever it was necessary to implement active cooperation projects with cities or regions, local Russian specialists were attracted primarily on a permanent basis. Thus, for example, a leading program specialist heads a small Vladimir-based group of three individuals who are implementing the program in Vladimir, in neighboring Ivanovo and Kostroma, and in Nizhni Novgorod oblast and Ryazan (in each of the last two places, a Russian specialist is also working permanently).

Adherence to these personnel policies has helped to ensure not only effective cooperation with the Russian Federation, municipalities, and private structures, but have paved the way for the institutionalization of the program, including creation of the Russian Institute for Urban Economics.

Notes

1. In Ekaterinburg and Novosibirsk, the work under the USAID contract was subsequently carried out by PADCO.

2. This phrase refers primarily to Saint-Petersburg. For a number of reasons, after the contract was signed, implementation of the program in this city was characterized by low interest on the part of some authorized officials. However, high-ranking officials in the city administration always expressed deep interest in obtaining technical assistance for housing reform when the expediency of continuing assistance was discussed.

3. Strange as it may seem, most decisions taken by governmental bodies in Russia are not made on the basis of prior calculations, though the need for these is recognized. Development of the methods for obtaining the necessary data, preparation of the appropriate software, and sofware distribution and training of users have always been core aspects of the HSRP.

4. The findings are summarized in Angelici, Struyk, and Tikhomirova (1995).

5. The results were discussed at a seminar presented in Moscow in July 1994 and were published in a special issue of the journal of the Russian Academy of Sciences, Voprosy ekonomiki, no. 10, October 1994, which distributed about 12,000 copies. The English translation is in Makhova and Struyk (1995).

SYNOPSES OF WORK STATEMENTS FOR SELECTED USAID/RUSSIA PROJECTS

1. Land and Real Estate Information Systems in Russia

CONTRACTOR: CHEMONICS

Project Summary: The objective of the project was to spur the creation and development of real estate markets by making available integrated and reliable information on real property title and encumbrances. Important related goals were to ensure that the benefits of private land and real property ownership are known and to create a cadre of Russians capable of designing, installing, and maintaining integrated real estate information systems—registries or simply information systems. Demonstration models were to be created in as many as 13 cities and 2 rural districts. It was anticipated that the project would take about nine months to complete. Multiple teams were expected to be working simultaneously at different sites.

This project was one of several carried out under the real estate component of USAID's privatization program. The task order for this project was signed in May 1994, although preliminary studies were done prior to the signing.

2. Market Environment Activities, Economic Restructuring, and Financial Sector Reform

CONTRACTOR: IRIS CENTER

Project Summary: This project was undertaken pursuant to a request from the Working Center for Economic Reform of the Russian Federation (WCER) to USAID for assistance of leading experts on regulation of natural monopolies. The specific tasks assigned to the contractor included:

a. Assisting the WCER in development of a Policy Analysis Unit on natural monopolies to undertake the formulation and evaluation of policy options for regulatory reform in specific sectors.

b. Working with the Policy Analysis Unit on the following activities:

- Preparation of brief diagnostic summaries of the current situation of industries or sectors considered to be natural monopolies;
- Beginning with the industries identified under the previous task as having the highest priority, formulating proposals for the design and implementation of industry-specific regulatory regimes for natural monopoly industries;
- Providing advice, technical assistance, and training to the recently formed Federal Energy Commission, one or two regional energy commissions, and similar federal and regional sectoral commissions established to regulate the activities of other natural monopoly industries, as needed and requested by the relevant commissions.

The contractor was to work with the WCER to accomplish all of these goals. Up to three resident expatriate advisors were provided for in the terms of reference. The overall project officially began in August 1994. USAID issues task directives for specific work under the overall contract.

3. Russian Federation Health Sector Reform Project

CONTRACTOR: ABT ASSOCIATES

Project Summary: This program's central purpose was to establish local, *raion-* (district-) based "working models" of modern health care systems that integrate new service delivery and financing methods, based on decades of innovation and experimentation in health care reform from around the world. The project was to demonstrate the feasibility of the following reforms:

- Diversification of funding sources;
- Creation of incentive-based provider payment systems;
- Improved, more cost-efficient service delivery;
- Privatization of facilities and group practices; and
- Improved quality of health care services, particularly in polyclinics.

The project's action plan called for activities in five areas to achieve these reforms:

1. Legal and regulatory reform; and
2. Demonstration projects in:

   a. Quality improvement;
   b. Financing and resource management;

   c. Information management; and
   d. Dissemination of findings.

The project's demonstrations were carried out initially and primarily in four Siberian regions (*oblasts*). In addition to the standard technical assistance elements, the projects included a substantial ($3 million) grants program for local entities to stimulate innovation. The project contract was signed in December 1993.

4. Municipal Finance and Management Project

CONTRACTOR: RESEARCH TRIANGLE INSTITUTE, INC.

Project Summary: This project was formulated to improve management and financial practices in as many as eight cities among several countries of the former Soviet Union (FSU). The Russian cities of Moscow and Nizhni Novgorod were specified as the first two in which activities would be initiated. The contract was signed in October 1993.

The general objective of the project was to introduce modern financial practices commonly used in the West, modified as appropriate for conditions and conventions in Russia or other FSU countries. The financial management improvement program was to include accounting, budgeting, financial planning, property tax administration, personnel management, and auditing systems.

The principal tasks of the project in Moscow and Nizhni Novgorod included:

1. Development and implementation of all central financial management systems;
2. Development of systems for the level of government immediately below the city level—that is, the district—and implementation in a selected number of these districts subject to budgetary constraints;
3. Development and implementation of financial systems in one city department (e.g., health, education); and
4. Assistance to one municipal enterprise (e.g., water, solid waste management) to develop and implement improved systems.

The project included substantial training for local government officials and the procurement of necessary computers and other equipment, in addition to technical advice and systems development. The contract explicitly stated the expectation that there would be close collaboration between the contractor and local officials.

5. Energy-Efficiency–Related Activities and Preparation of a Transmission Project as a Follow-Up to the Joint Energy Alternatives Study

CONTRACTOR: BURNS AND ROE

Project Summary: As its title indicates, this project grew out of a joint Russian-American study on the development of a long-term, comprehensive investment program for the Russian power sector. The study was conducted under the so-called Chernomyrdin-Gore process.

The project actually consists of a set of discrete tasks in the power sector as follows:

1. District heating efficiency improvement. Under this task a comprehensive program was to be developed and implemented. The work was to involve determining the economics of technical retrofits for efficiency improvement to district heating systems and reviewing the institutional and financial barriers to proposed remedies; providing assistance to a multilateral lender in preparing a loan for district heating energy efficiency improvement; assisting in the development of capability, primarily in the private sector, to provide energy-efficient services to district heating enterprises, including assistance in forming an association of energy engineers; and the design and initial offering of relevant training courses.
2. Natural gas distribution. This task was to develop and analyze data on the use of natural gas in single family homes. The project team was to organize the installation of meters in 500 units in each of two cities, monitor the collection of data, and analyze the data. The activity was in support of a World Bank loan project.
3. Preparations for transmission project to support development bank lending. The project team was to perform the detailed analytical and design work to facilitate appraisal of the second power sector loan by the World Bank for Russia.

In addition to the activities just listed, the contractor was to carry out certain tasks in conjunction with the U.S. government's Commodity Import Program, under which substantial quantities of energy audit equipment were being imported to Russia.

The contract for this work was signed in October 1993. The initial contract was for two and one-half years, with a two-and-one-half-year optional extension. USAID excercised the option and the project is now scheduled to conclude in 1998.

OVERVIEW OF U.S. ASSISTANCE PROGRAMS IN THE FORMER SOVIET BLOC

by Clare Romanik

The U.S. Congress first authorized aid for Poland and Hungary through the Support for East European Democracy Act (SEED), signed by President George Bush on November 28, 1989. Czechoslovakia was soon added to the beneficiaries list, and other Central and Eastern European (CEE) countries followed as their former regimes toppled and they looked to the West for guidance and aid. Since fiscal year 1993, obligations for programs in the region have been funded under both the SEED Act and the Foreign Assistance Act of 1961 (as amended, PL 87-195) (GAO 1995c).

Some assistance was provided to the Soviet Union as early as December 1990, and in 1991 Congress authorized the U.S. Department of Defense to establish a Cooperative Threat Reduction program. After the breakup of the Soviet Union in December 1991, Congress increased assistance to the Newly Independent States (NIS) and formally established a general program through the enactment of the Freedom Support Act[1] in October 1992 (GAO, 1995c: 2).

The key objectives of these programs have evolved somewhat over time. According to a 1991 GAO report, the key objectives to be promoted by the U.S. assistance program in Eastern Europe were: (1) progress toward political pluralism, (2) progress toward economic reform, (3) enhanced respect for human rights, and (4) friendly relations with the United States (GAO 1991a: 4). The 1996 report by the coordinator for SEED Assistance states objectives that differ somewhat from the original ones:

- Development of a market economy and a strong private sector;
- Development and strengthening of institutions necessary for sustainable democracy; and
- Improvement of the basic quality of life in selected areas.

Similar objectives were given by the coordinator for assistance to the NIS for the program in Russia:

- A competitive, efficient, market-oriented economy in which the majority of economic resources are privately owned and managed and economic decisions are based primarily on individual choice.
- Transparent and accountable governance, the empowerment of citizens working through civic and economic organizations and democratic political processes to ensure broad-based participation in political and economic life, and respect for human rights, fundamental freedoms, and the rule of law.
- An enhanced capacity to manage the human dimension of the economic and political transition, to deliver social services in a sustainable fiscal framework and market environment, and to improve the quality of life for all citizens, with particular concern for vulnerable groups. (Coordinator of U.S. Assistance to the Newly Independent States 1995).

The biggest change over the years in the programs' objectives is the recognition that improving quality of life should play an important role in U.S. assistance efforts. The redefined objectives also explicitly include governance and the development of institutions. Early reviews of the programs in Central and Eastern Europe faulted them for focusing too much on the private sector at the expense of institutional development for the newly constituted governments (GAO 1991a, 1992). The greater emphasis on institutions and the decision also to target human issues (that are addressed by governments, not the private sector) may have been a response to these earlier criticisms.

Initially, assistance to Eastern Europe was to be delivered in three stages:

- Short-term assistance, which is humanitarian aid (food and medicine);
- Medium-term assistance, which is to support democratic institutions and includes (1) technical assistance and training and (2) normalization of bilateral trade and investment relations; and
- Long-term assistance, which is to help host countries to institutionalize political and economic reforms, and includes (1) supporting stabilization and structural adjustment programs and providing enterprise funds for private-sector development, (2) bringing the countries into the world economy through membership in international trade and financial institutions, (3) providing access to high technology through relaxation of controls over sensitive exports, and (4) participating in the European Bank for Reconstruction and Development (GAO 1991a: 4).

According to schedule, the first stage consisting of humanitarian aid programs has mostly been completed.[2] Some technical assistance programs, namely in the Czech Republic and Estonia, will be phased out by 1996 and 1997. However, the time horizon of "medium-term assistance" in other countries, particularly of the former Soviet Union, has been extended until the end of the century. Long-term assistance efforts also continue, including the creation and promotion of enterprise funds.[3] In keeping with the primary U.S. focus on the private sector, enterprise funds received authorization in the initial assistance legislation and have program end dates that extend to the beginning of the next century (see table C.2).

Both the CEE and NIS programs have a special coordinating office within the U.S. Department of State with responsibility for providing overall policy guidance and monitoring as well as for setting project funding levels for aid to the region (GAO 1995c: 44). However, it is the

Table C.1 U.S. ASSISTANCE TO FORMER SOVIET UNION: OBLIGATIONS AND EXPENDITURES BY PROGRAM AREA, NONCREDIT PROGRAMS (FY 1990–DECEMBER 31, 1994) (DOLLARS IN THOUSANDS)

Program area	Obligations ($)	Percent of total obligations	Expenditures ($)	Percent of total expenditures
Food Aid	1,548,559	28.83	1,446,576	41.45
Private-Sector Development	765,735	14.26	307,081	8.80
Emergency Humanitarian Assistance	608,910	11.34	574,704	16.47
Weapons of Mass Destruction	367,655	6.85	88,290	2.53
Democratic Reform	306,701	5.71	187,052	5.36
Energy	289,662	5.39	129,337	3.71
Other	269,177	5.01	252,544	7.24
Space Research	227,553	4.24	112,888	3.23
Exchanges and Training	188,324	3.51	109,928	3.15
Environment	187,596	3.49	72,189	2.07
Resettlement for Military Officers/Housing	172,447	3.21	16,008	0.46
Food Systems Improvement	111,132	2.07	49,381	1.42
Economic Restructuring and Finance	110,089	2.05	51,473	1.48
Health Care Improvement	87,537	1.63	41,296	1.18
Defense Conversion	72,838	1.36	14,300	0.41
U.S. Export Market Development	32,314	0.60	12,487	0.36
Scientific Research Awards	21,432	0.40	20,831	0.60
Military Education and Training	3,303	0.06	3,303	0.09
Total	5,370,964	100.00	3,489,668	100.00

Source: U.S. General Accounting Office (1996).

Table C.2 U.S. ASSISTANCE TO FORMER SOVIET UNION: USAID NONCREDIT
PROGRAM OBLIGATIONS AND EXPENDITURES BY PROGRAM
(FY 1990–DECEMBER 31, 1994) (DOLLARS IN THOUSANDS)

Program	Obligations ($)	Expenditures ($)	Program end date
Central Asian-American Enterprise Fund	30,000	1,290	6/1/00
Democratic Pluralism	122,636	47,540	12/31/99
Disaster Assistance	6,342	4,532	To be determined
Economic Restructuring and Financial Sector Reform	72,171	24,121	9/30/98
Energy Efficiency and Market Reform	184,403	24,651	2/25/99
Environmental Policy and Technology	67,173	16,513	9/30/99
Eurasia Foundation	26,000	21,069	4/30/97
European Bank for Reconstruction and Development Enterprise Fund	29,000	4,300	6/1/00
Exchanges and Training	99,113	49,863	12/30/99
Farmer-to-Farmer	30,160	21,430	9/95
Food Systems Restructuring	60,837	21,377	9/30/97
Funds for Large Enterprises in Russia	40,000	15,300	6/1/00
Health Care Improvement	83,097	37,259	12/31/98
Housing Sector Reform	207,567	36,949	11/30/96
Humanitarian Assistance for Armenian Earthquake Victims	9,909	9,868	Completed 9/30/94
Humanitarian Emergency Medical Supply for the Soviet Union	10,000	10,000	Completed 9/30/93
NIS Special Initiatives	181,700	140,812	9/30/97
Private-Sector Initiatives	517,943	248,071	9/30/00
Russian-American Enterprise Fund	70,000	14,921	6/1/00
Russia Energy and Environment Commodities Import Program	90,000	0	12/13/95
Western NIS Enterprise Fund	45,000	1,525	6/1/00
Total	1,983,051	851,391	

Source: U.S. General Accounting Office (1996).

Bureau for Europe and the Newly Independent States within the United States Agency for International Development (USAID) that implements the majority of programs. Other agencies involved include the departments of Agriculture, Commerce, Defense, and Energy; the United States Information Agency; the Environmental Protection Agency; the Trade and Development Agency; the Peace Corps; and the Overseas Private Investment Corporation. The National Aeronautics

Table C.3 U.S. ASSISTANCE TO FORMER SOVIET UNION: IMPLEMENTING AGENCY FOR NONCREDIT PROGRAMS
(FY 1990–DECEMBER 31, 1994) (DOLLARS IN THOUSANDS)

Agency	Obligations ($)	Percent of total obligations	Expenditures ($)	Percent of obligations expended
U.S. Agency for International Development	1,983,051	36.92	851,391	42.93
Department of Agriculture	1,638,660	30.51	1,577,006	96.24
Department of Defense	823,282	15.33	482,772	58.64
National Aeronautics and Space Administration	235,296	4.38	117,830	50.08
Department of Energy	231,035	4.30	122,535	53.04
U.S. Information Agency	219,326	4.08	162,427	74.06
Department of State	83,751	1.56	70,848	84.59
Peace Corps	33,813	0.63	32,908	97.32
Trade and Development Agency	31,274	0.58	11,447	36.60
Department of Health and Human Services	23,512	0.44	22,629	96.24
Department of Commerce	22,796	0.42	9,020	39.57
Treasury Department	11,095	0.21	6,006	54.13
Department of the Interior	8,397	0.16	2,118	25.22
Nuclear Regulatory Commission	6,950	0.13	4,142	59.60
National Science Foundation	6,377	0.12	6,377	100.00
Environmental Protection Agency	6,145	0.11	5,682	92.47
Overseas Private Investment Corporation	2,814	0.05	1,881	66.84
Department of Transportation	1,407	0.03	1,229	87.35
Arms Control and Disarmament Agency	814	0.02	598	73.46
Congressional Research Service	721	0.01	375	52.01
Department of Justice	414	0.01	414	100.00
Securities and Exchange Commission	34	0.00	33	97.06
Total	5,370,964	100.00	3,489,668	64.97

Source: U.S. General Accounting Office (1996).

and Space Administration is also involved in assistance to the NIS (see table C.3).

Agencies provide aid for the sector in which they have particular expertise, and participate in the planning process through sectoral working groups. "The sectoral working groups bring together relevant agencies with staff from the State Department Coordinator's Office to develop detailed program plans for sectors and proposed projects within programs" (GAO 1995d: 19). However, a 1995 GAO report on U.S. assistance to the NIS highlighted how the 22 providing agencies lacked coordination and the agency often disputed the appropriateness of the programs and the management style (ibid).[4]

Originally, almost all management of USAID programs was handled by the Washington, D.C.–based bureau. In response to criticisms, however, USAID increased its presence in the recipient countries and has been able to shift substantial responsibility to the field offices. At the same time, the programs have become more tailored to individual countries, whereas some regional-level programs continue. In the beginning of 1996, there were 12 USAID offices in Central and Eastern

Table C.4 U.S. BILATERAL CREDIT/INSURANCE PROGRAMS WITH FORMER SOVIET UNION
(FY 1991–DECEMBER 31, 1994) (DOLLARS IN THOUSANDS)

Agency	Program	Definition of face value	Face value ($)	Subsidy cost ($)
OPIC	Loan guarantee	Value of commitment	838,300	36,928
OPIC	Insurance	Value of policy committed to project	983,860	N.A.[a]
Eximbank	Loan guarantee	Value of final commitment	1,757,829	315,469
Eximbank	Direct loans	Value of final commitment	88,764	17,295
Eximbank	Insurance	Value of goods shipped under policy	586,530	0[b]
USDA	Food aid loans	Total loan amount	693,900	457,333
USDA	GSM-102 loan guarantees	Registration amount	5,031,016	254,267
Total			9,980,199	1,081,292

Source: U.S. General Accounting Office (1996).
Note: Credit subsidy cost is estimated long-term cost to U.S. government of providing loans or guarantees calculated on a net present value basis.
a. Subsidy cost does not apply to OPIC insurance program because it does not fall under Credit Reform requirements.
b. Credit Reform requirements apply to Eximbank insurance program. However, Eximbank cannot calculate subsidy figures for its insurance program on a per-country basis, and as such, could not provide subsidy figures for its insurance program in the former Soviet Union.

Europe. For the NIS, it was decided to consolidate resources in four missions with each serving multiple countries.[5] The USAID staff in the region is too small to carry out the extensive programs; rather, they manage intermediaries such as contractors, universities, and private voluntary organizations in their program activities.

For FY 1990–95, the SEED Act funded approximately $2.2 billion in programs for Central and East European countries.[6] From 1990 to 1994, $5.4 billion in obligations were funded for noncredit NIS programs, but only $3.4 billion were expended for the same period. At close to $2 billion, USAID had the largest obligations of any implementing agency, but in actual expenditures it was second to the Department of Agriculture (see table C.3).

In comparing the value of U.S. noncredit and credit programs, one could come to different conclusions depending on how the latter are measured. For example, the total subsidy cost of bilateral credit agreements and insurance that the United States provided countries of the former Soviet Union from 1990 to the end of 1994 is $1.1 billion (see table C.4). This is less than one-third of expenditures on noncredit NIS programs during the same period. On the other hand, at face value these credit agreements and insurance are worth approximately $10 billion, which is close to three times the expenditures on noncredit NIS programs (GAO 1996).

Until 1993, Poland was the largest recipient of U.S. assistance in the region. In fact, in 1991 it received almost 90 percent of U.S. bilateral assistance to the region because of its debt forgiveness program (DAC/OECD 1996: 63).[7] Russia has since taken its place; from 1990 to 1994 it received close to half of the U.S. bilateral assistance to the NIS (see table C.5). Whereas the absolute levels of aid for Russia far overshadow other countries, its per capita assistance levels are more modest. Among the 12 NIS countries, U.S. per capita expenditures on noncredit programs in Russia from 1990 to 1994 ($11.21) ranked eighth. Far higher per capita expenditures were received by countries with much smaller populations such as Armenia, Georgia, and Kyrgyzstan. The range of per capita SEED assistance levels for CEE countries is not as large as the range of per capita expenditures in the NIS countries (see table C.6).

Notes

1. The act's official title is the Freedom for Russia and Emerging Eurasian Democracies and Open Markets Support Act of 1992 (PL 102-511).

Table C.5 U.S. ASSISTANCE TO FORMER SOVIET UNION: EXPENDITURES BY
COUNTRY, NONCREDIT PROGRAMS
(FY 1990–DECEMBER 31, 1994)

Country	Expenditures per capita ($)	Total expenditures (thousands $)	Percent of total expenditures
Russia	11.21	1,661,064	47.60
Armenia	96.80	350,897	10.06
FSU-wide	N.A.	258,330	7.40
Ukraine	4.91	253,794	7.27
Georgia	44.82	243,301	6.97
Kyrgyzstan	34.86	156,012	4.47
Belarus	13.27	136,677	3.92
Kazakhstan	7.68	128,201	3.67
Moldova	15.79	68,772	1.97
Tajikstan	11.26	64,235	1.84
Turkmenistan	16.05	63,909	1.83
Azerbaijan	7.00	52,198	1.50
Uzbekistan	1.47	32,608	0.93
Soviet Union	N.A.	12,527	0.36
Non-Russia FSU[a]	N.A.	4,716	0.14
Nuclear Weapon States[b]	N.A.	2,429	0.07
Total		3,489,668	100.00

Source: U.S. General Accounting Office (1996).
Note: N.A., data not available.
a. Expenditures for programs for which the agency could not provide a specific country breakout, but knew that nothing was expended for Russia.
b. Russia, Ukraine, Belarus, and Kazakhstan.

2. The expenditures-to-obligations ratios for NIS programs confirm this. As of December 31, 1994, food aid and emergency humanitarian assistance had expenditures over 90 percent of obligations, while most other program areas had expenditure levels less than 50 percent of obligations (see table C.1).

3. "The enterprise funds are private U.S. corporations authorized by Congress and staffed by experienced business managers. . . . [They] primarily make loans to, or investments in, small and medium business in which other financial institutions are reluctant to invest" (GAO 1994: 2).

4. In response to this and other criticisms, President Bill Clinton strengthened the role and authority of the coordinator in April 1995. His new title is special advisor to the president and to the secretary of state on assistance to the former Soviet Union. Implementing agencies are directed to bring all programs and budget plans for such assistance and activities to the coordinator (GAO 1995a: 3).

5. The USAID mission in Almaty (Kazakhstan) coordinates Central Asian programs; the Yerevan (Armenia) mission coordinates programs in the Caucasus and the Kiev mission programs in the Slavic countries except for Russia. The Moscow mission coordinates programs for the Russian Federation as well as NIS-wide programs.

Table C.6 SEED ASSISTANCE TO CENTRAL AND EAST EUROPE:
OBLIGATIONS BY COUNTRY
(FY 1990–1995)

Country	Obligations per capita ($)	Total obligations (thousands $)	Percent of total obligations
Poland	21.0	805,480	36.5
Regional/Unspecified	N.A.	263,008	11.9
Hungary	21.3	217,017	9.8
Bulgaria	19.9	176,731	8.0
Romania	6.5	148,129	6.7
Czech Republic	14.0	144,673	6.5
Slovak Republic	26.5	140,266	6.3
Albania	29.9	101,584	4.6
Lithuania	11.9	44,060	2.0
Bosnia	N.A.	34,500	1.6
Latvia	12.8	33,314	1.5
FYROM (Macedonia)	15.4	32,376	1.5
Croatia	N.A.	28,560	1.3
Estonia	16.2	25,928	1.2
Slovenia	4.9	9,371	0.4
Yugoslavia	N.A.	2,476	0.1
Total		2,207,473	100.0

Source: U.S. Department of State (1996).
Note: N.A., data not available.

6. The figure of $2.2 billion does not include funds for credit programs or for agency CEE programs that are not SEED funded, such as USDA food aid ($653 million) and USAID disaster relief ($374 million).

7. Over half of U.S. assistance to Poland from 1990 to September 1994 came in the form of official debt forgiveness ($2.4 billion). Less than one-fifth ($719 million) was devoted to assistance programs (GAO, 1995e).

Table C.7 SEED ASSISTANCE TO CENTRAL AND EAST EUROPE:
OBLIGATIONS BY OBJECTIVE
(FY 1990–1995) (DOLLARS IN THOUSANDS)

Objective	Total obligations ($)	Percent of total obligations
Strengthening Democratic Institutions		
Political Process and Governance	87,388	4.0
Democratic Pluralism	77,025	3.5
Economic Restructuring		
Macroeconomic Support	234,140	10.6
Privatization and Assistance to Enterprises	283,352	12.8
Improving the Business Climate	109,145	4.9
Investment and Trade	492,486	22.3
Human Resources	148,836	6.7
Agriculture and Agribusiness	116,022	5.3
Agriculture Sector Programs	48,156	2.2
Energy Efficiency	119,187	5.4
Improving the Quality of Life		
Short-term Emergency and Humanitarian Aid	116,585	5.3
Employment and the Social Safety Net	31,033	1.4
Housing	76,601	3.5
Health	68,162	3.1
Environment	123,210	5.6
Miscellaneous	76,142	3.4
Total	2,207,473	100.0

Source: U.S. Department of State (1996).
Notes: Tables C.6 and C.7 only include funds budgeted by SEED. Several agencies (such as Peace Corps, USIA, USDA, and DOD) have CEE programs that are not SEED funded. Other U.S. assistance initiatives and programs include: Food Assistance and Credit Guarantees ($1.2 billion); USDA Emerging Democracies Program ($10 million annually); Scientific Cooperation Program ($0.6 million); Department of Defense's Excess Property Program ($5.8 million); and USAID Disaster Relief ($374 million). In addition, the Overseas Private Investment Corporation has provided financing and insurance worth over $2 billion; the U.S. Trade and Development Agency has provided $39 million in funding over SEED transfers; and Eximbank has provided credit insurance and loan guarantees in most CEE countries.

PROJECT EVALUATIONS REVIEWED FOR CHAPTER TWO

Baser, Fred R., and Paul Holmes. 1992. *The World Environment Center Central and Eastern Europe Program: An Evaluation of Cooperative Agreement No. ANE-0004-A-00-0048-00*. Submitted to U.S. Agency for International Development.

Foster, Barbara Barrett, David A. Grossman, and April L. Young. 1994. *Phase I: Local Government Program Evaluation: Democracy Activities in Poland and Bulgaria*. Prepared for U.S. Agency for International Development, September 30.

U.S. General Accounting Office. 1995. *Foreign Assistance: Assessment of Selected USAID Projects in Russia*, August. (Agribusiness Partnerships Project/Tri Valley Growers; Commercial Real Estate Project/International Business and Technical Consultants, Inc.; District Heating Project/RCG Haggler Bailly; Environmental Policy and Technology Project/CH2M Hill International Services; Health Care Training Project/Partners for International Education and Training.)

Hobgood, Harlan, Mary Muller, and Karl Van Orsdol. 1995. *Evaluation of the Environmental Training Project in Central and Eastern Europe*. Report submitted to ENI/EEUD/ENR U.S. Agency for International Development, January 15.

Merrill, Sally R., Antony Phipps, Harry Garnett, and Mariam Maxian. 1993. *Mid-Term Evaluation of the Eastern Europe Housing and Urban Program*. Submitted to Office of Housing and Urban Programs, U.S. Agency for International Development, July.

Privatization Phase II Program Evaluation (Contract No. 180-0014). 1993. Submitted to EUR/PDP/PA U.S. Agency for International Development by a Joint Venture, Development Economics Group/Louis Berger International, Inc., & Checchi and Company Consulting, Inc., July 30.

Regional Inspector General for Audit in Bonn, USAID. 1993. *Audit of the Department of Labor's Technical Assistance Activities in Bulgaria*, August 12.

————. 1993. *Audit of the Department of Commerce's Special American Business Internship Training Program in the New Independent States*, September 24.

————. 1993. *Audit of the Department of Labor's Technical Assistance Activities in Poland*, November 15.

————. 1994. *Audit of the Department of Treasury's Technical Assistance Activities in Bulgaria*, February 25.

Scientech. 1994. *Evaluation of the Impact of the Industrial Energy Component of the Emergency Energy Project*. 1994. Submitted to ENI/ODR/EID U.S. Agency for International Development, June.

REFERENCES

Abt Associates. 1995. "Russian Federation Health Sector Reform Project, Country Action Plan & Progress, 1995–1996: Executive Summary," Moscow: Abt Project Office Report to USAID.

Angelici, K., R. Struyk, and M. Tikhomirova. 1995. "Private Maintenance for Moscow's Municipal Housing Stock: Does It Work?" *Journal of Housing* 4(1): 50–70.

Assaf, George B. 1994. "Technical Assistance Toward Restructuring and Privatization in Central and Eastern Europe." *East-Central European Economies in Transition: Study Papers Submitted to the Joint Economic Committee, Congress of the United States* (November): 239–258.

Barre, Raymond, William H. Luers, Anthony Solomon, and Krzysztof J. Ners. 1992. *Moving Beyond Assistance.* New York: Institute for East West Studies.

Baser, F. and P. Holmes. 1992. "An Evaluation of Cooperative Agreement No. ANE-0004-A-00-0048-00," Report to USAID Bureau for Europe and Newly Independent States and The World Environment Center.

Berlage, Lodewijk and Olav Stokke. 1991. "Evaluating Development Assistance: State of the Art and Main Challenges Ahead." In *Evaluating Development Assistance: Approaches and Methods*, edited by Berlage and Stokke (1–32). London: Frank Cass & Co. Ltd.

Breslauer, G. 1995. "Aid to Russia: What Difference Can Western Policy Make?" In *The New Russia: Troubled Transformation*, edited by Gail Lapidus (223–244). Boulder: Westview Press.

Brinkerhoff, D.W. 1994. "Institutional Development in World Bank Projects: Analytical Approaches and Intervention Designs," *Public Administration and Development* 14: 135–141.

Butler, S., O. Kaganova, A. Khakhalin, Y. Lipeskih, O. Stoloff, T. Sukhorukoua, and A. Vysokovsky. 1996. "Land for Housing: Urban Land Privatization Demonstration Project." Moscow: Urban Institute Technical Cooperation Office, processed.

Buyck, Beatrice. 1991. "The Bank's Use of Technical Assistance for Institutional Development." World Bank Staff Working Papers No. 578. Washington, DC: World Bank.

Cassen, R. and associates. 1994. *Does Aid Work?* 2nd Edition. Oxford: Clarendon Press.

CCET/OECD. 1994. *Comparative Assessment of Key Technical Assistance to the Partners in Transition and Four New Independent States of the Former Soviet Union*, November 11.

Cohen, M. 1983. *Learning By Doing: World Bank Lending for Urban Development, 1979–82.* Washington, DC: The World Bank.

Competellor, John. 1995. "Audit of Selected Privatization and Restructuring Activities in Russia (Project No. 110-0005), Audit Report No. 8-118-95-007." Memo to Barbara Turner, DAA/PA. March 10.

Coordinator of U.S. Assistance to the Newly Independent States. 1995. *United States Assistance and Economic Cooperation Strategy for Russia,* February 3.

DAC/OECD. 1991. *DAC's Principles for New Orientations in Technical Cooperation.*

DAC/OECD. 1996. *Assistance Programmes for Central and Eastern Europe and the Former Soviet Union.*

Daschle, T. 1996. "The Water's Edge," *Foreign Policy* (103): 3–19.

Development Economics Group/Louis Berger International, Inc. & Checchi and Company Consulting, Inc. 1993. "Privatization Phase II Program Evaluation (Contract No. 180-0014)" Submitted to EUR/PDP/PA U.S. Agency for International Development, July 30.

European Commission Directorate General IA. 1995. *Scoreboard of Assistance Commitments to the Countries of Central and Eastern Europe, 1990–1994,* March.

Foster, B. Barrett, D. Grossman, A. Young. 1994. "Phase 1, Local Government Program Evaluation: Democracy Activities in Poland and Bulgaria." Arlington, VA: Technical Support Services, Report to USAID Office of Democracy Initiatives.

Greenberger, R.S. 1995. "Dateline Capitol Hill: The New Majority's Foreign Policy," *Foreign Policy* (101): 159–169.

Hobgood, H., M. Muller, K. Van Orsdol. 1995. "Evaluation of the Environmental Training Project in Central and Eastern Europe." Burlington, VT: Associates in Rural Development, Inc., Report to USAID Bureau for Europe and Newly Independent States.

Hoffman, M., M. Koleva, G. Valais, D. Kavrakov, and A. Zarr. 1996. "Local Government Initiative: Revised Work Plan." Washington, DC: Urban Institute Report prepared for the U.S. Agency for International Development, processed.

Hutchings, Robert L. 1994. "Five Years After: Reflections on the Post-Communist Transitions and Western Assistance Strategies," *East-Central European Economies in Transition: Study Papers Submitted to the Joint Economic Committee, Congress of the United States* (November): 176–190.

Keay, J. 1995. "Consultants in Eastern Europe Say They Aren't to Blame for Projects' Failures," *International Herald Tribune*, October 16: 11.

Kosareva, N., A. Puzanov, and A. Suchkov. 1996. "Russia: Fast Starter," in R. Struyk (ed.) *Economic Restructuring in the Former Soviet Bloc: The Case of Housing*. Washington, DC: Urban Institute Press: 255–306.

Kull, S. 1995. "What the Public Knows that Washington Doesn't," *Foreign Policy* (101): 102–115.

Lawrence, P., and C. Vlachoutsicous. 1993. "Joint Ventures in Russia: Put the Locals in Charge," *Harvard Business Review* (Jan.–Feb.): 44–54.

Layard, R., and J. Parker. 1996. *The Coming Russian Boom: A Guide to New Markets and Politics*. New York: Free Press.

Lee, L., and C. Romanik. 1995. "The Moscow Housing Household Survey: Description of the Sample." Moscow: Urban Institute Technical Co-operation Office, processed.

Lethem, F. and L. Cooper. 1983. "Managing Project-Related Technical Assistance—the Lessons for Success." World Bank Staff Working Paper No. 586. Washington, DC: World Bank.

Makhova, Y., and R. Struyk. 1995. *Urban Housing Markets in Russia: Translation of a Special Issue of the Russian Journal, Voprosi Ekonomiki*, Issue 10, 1994. Moscow: Urban Institute Technical Cooperation Office.

Merrill, S., A. Phipps, H. Garnett, M. Maxian. 1993. "Mid-Term Evaluation of the Eastern Europe Housing and Urban Program."Cambridge, MA: Abt Associates, Report to USAID Office of Housing and Urban Programs.

Mosley, Paul. 1992. "Evaluating the Effectiveness of Technical Cooperation Expenditures." In *Evaluating Development Assistance: Approaches and Methods*, edited by Berlage and Stokke (73–84). London: Frank Cass & Co. Ltd.

Muscat, R.J. 1986. "Evaluating Technical Cooperation: A Review of the Literature." *Development Policy Review* 4: 69–88.

O'Leary, S., S. Butler, I. Dmitrieva, R. Pinegina, and R. Struyk. 1996. "Russian Enterprise Housing Divestiture." Washington, DC: The Urban Institute.

Pchelintsev O., T. Belkina, and T. Tcherbakova. 1994. "Housing Indicators for Moscow: 1989–1993." Moscow: Institute for Economic Forecasting, processed.

Puzanov, A.S. 1996. "Transfer to the New System of Housing Payments and Introduction of Housing Allowances in the Russian Federation in 1994–1995: Results and Problems." Moscow: Urban Institute Technical Cooperation Program, processed.

Quigley, K. 1995. "Spring into Summer: The Role of Private Foundations in Extending Public Debate in Central and Eastern Europe." In *Beyond Government: Extending the Public Policy Debate in Emerging Democracies*, edited by C.D. Goodwin and M. Nacht (405–422). Boulder: Westview Press.

Rapaczynski, A. 1996. "The Roles of the State and Market in Establishing Property Rights," *Journal of Economic Perspectives* 10(2): 87–103.

Regional Inspector General for Audit in Bonn, USAID. 1993a. *Audit of the Department of Labor's Technical Assistance Activities in Bulgaria,* August 12.

————. 1993b. *Audit of the Department of Commerce's Special American Business Internship Training Program in the New Independent States,* September 24.

————. 1993c. *Audit of the Department of Labor's Technical Assistance Activities in Poland,* November 15.

————. 1994. *Audit of the Distribution of Emergency Medical Supplies to the New Independent States under USAID Cooperative Agreement with the People-to-People Health Foundation 'Project Hope',* March 17.

Renard, Robrecht and Lodewijk Berlage. 1992. "The Rise and Fall of Cost-Benefit Analysis in Developing Countries." In *Evaluating Development Assistance: Approaches and Methods,* edited by Berlage and Stokke (33–55). London: Frank Cass & Co. Ltd.

Schiavo-Campo, Salvatore, ed. 1994. "Institutional Change and the Public Sector I Transitional Economies." World Bank Discussion Papers No. 241. Washington, DC: World Bank.

Scientech. 1994. "Evaluation of the Impact of the Industrial Energy-Efficient Component of the Emergency Energy Project," Idaho Falls, ID: Scientech, Report to USAID Bureau for Europe and Newly Independent States.

Siegel, Daniel and Jenny Yancey. *The Rebirth of Civil Society: The Development of the Nonprofit Sector in East Central Europe and the Role of Western Assistance.* Rockefeller Brothers Fund, Inc. New York: 1992.

Struyk, R., A. Puzanov, and L. Lee. 1996. "Monitoring Russia's Experience with Housing Allowances." Moscow: Urban Institute Technical Co-operation Office.

Struyk, R. 1994. "Delivering Technical Assistance in Eastern Europe and Russia: Notes from the Field," *Policy and Politics* 22(3): 203–210.

Struyk, R., N. Kosareva, J. Daniell, C. Hanson, and M. Mikelsons. 1993. *Implementing Housing Allowances in Russia: Rationalizing the Rental Sector.* Washington, DC: The Urban Institute Press.

Struyk, R., and A. Puzanov. 1995. "An Early Assessment of Russia's Housing Allowance Program." Moscow: Urban Institute Technical Cooperation Office, processed.

Sutela, P. 1991. *Economic Thought and Economic Reform in the Soviet Union.* Cambridge, U.K.: Cambridge University Press.

Thomas, S. 1995. "Grading U.S. Aid to Central and Eastern Europe," Paper presented at the seminar "Western Aid to Central and Eastern Europe: What We Are Doing Right, What We Are Doing Wrong, What

We Can Do Better," organized by the Woodrow Wilson International Center for Scholars, Washington, DC, Apr. 18–20.

U.S. Congress. 1994. Senate Foreign Relations Committee. *Assistance to the Newly Independent States: A Status Report.* S. PRT. 103-73. 103rd Cong., 2d sess., February.

U.S. Department of State. 1996. *SEED Act Implementation Report.* Washington, DC: February 29.

U.S. General Accounting Office. 1991a. *Eastern Europe: Donor Assistance and Reform Efforts.* GAO/NSIAD-91-21. Washington, DC: U.S. Government Printing Office.

_____. 1991b. *Eastern Europe: Status of U.S. Assistance Efforts.* GAO/NSIAD-91-110. Washington, DC: U.S. Government Printing Office.

_____. 1992. *Poland and Hungary: Economic Transition and U.S. Assistance.* GAO/NSIAD-92-102. Washington, DC: U.S. Government Printing Office.

_____. 1994. *Enterprise Funds: Evolving Models for Private Sector Development in Central and Eastern Europe.* GAO/NSIAD-94-77. Washington, DC: U.S. Government Printing Office.

_____. 1995a. *Foreign Assistance: Assessment of Selected USAID Projects in Russia.* GAO/NSIAD-95-156. Washington, DC: U.S. Government Printing Office.

_____. 1995b. *Foreign Assistance: Donors' Approaches for Managing AID Programs.* GAO/NSIAD-95-37. Washington, DC: U.S. Government Printing Office.

_____. 1995c. *Former Soviet Union. An Update on Coordination of U.S. Assistance and Economic Cooperation Programs.* GAO/NSIAD-96-16. Washington, DC: U.S. Government Printing Office.

_____. 1995d. *Former Soviet Union: U.S. Bilateral Program Lacks Effective Coordination.* GAO/NSIAD-95-110. Washington, DC: U.S. Government Printing Office.

_____. 1995e. *Poland: Economic Restructuring and Donor Assistance.* GAO/NSIAD-95-150. Washington, DC: U.S. Government Printing Office.

_____. 1996. *Former Soviet Union—Information on U.S. Bilateral Program Funding,* GAO/NSIAD-96-37. Washington, DC: U.S. Government Printing Office.

Waller, J.M. 1996. "To Russia, With Cash," *Reader's Digest,* June: 177–181.

Wedel, Janine R. 1994. "U.S. Aid to Central and Eastern Europe, 1990–1994: An Analysis of Aid Models and Responses," *East-Central European Economies in Transition: Study Papers Submitted to the Joint Economic Committee, Congress of the United States* (November): 299–335.

World Bank. 1982. *Review of Training in Bank-Financed Projects.* Washington, DC: The World Bank.

―――――. 1993. *Handbook on Technical Assistance*. Washington, DC: World Bank, Operations Policy Department.

―――――. 1996. "Performance Indicators for Technical Assistance Operations." Washington, DC.: World Bank, Operations Policy Department.

―――――. 1996a. *From Plan to Market: World Development Report 1996*. Oxford: Oxford University Press for the World Bank.

―――――. 1996b. "1994 Evaluation Report." Washington, DC: World Bank, Operations Evaluation Department.

ABOUT THE AUTHOR

Raymond J. Struyk, a senior fellow at the Urban Institute, is a senior analyst in the fields of housing policy, housing finance, and community development and has extensive policy formulation experience. He joined the Urban Institute in 1972. He has been at the Institute since then except for 27 months in 1977–1979 when he was the Deputy Assistant Secretary for Research at the Department of Housing and Urban Development. Among his many publications are *Clear and Convincing Evidence: Measurement of Discrimination in America*, coedited with Michael Fix (Urban Institute Press, 1993), and *Economic Restructuring of the Former Soviet Bloc: The Case of Housing* (Urban Institute Press, 1996).